The Lawn Bible

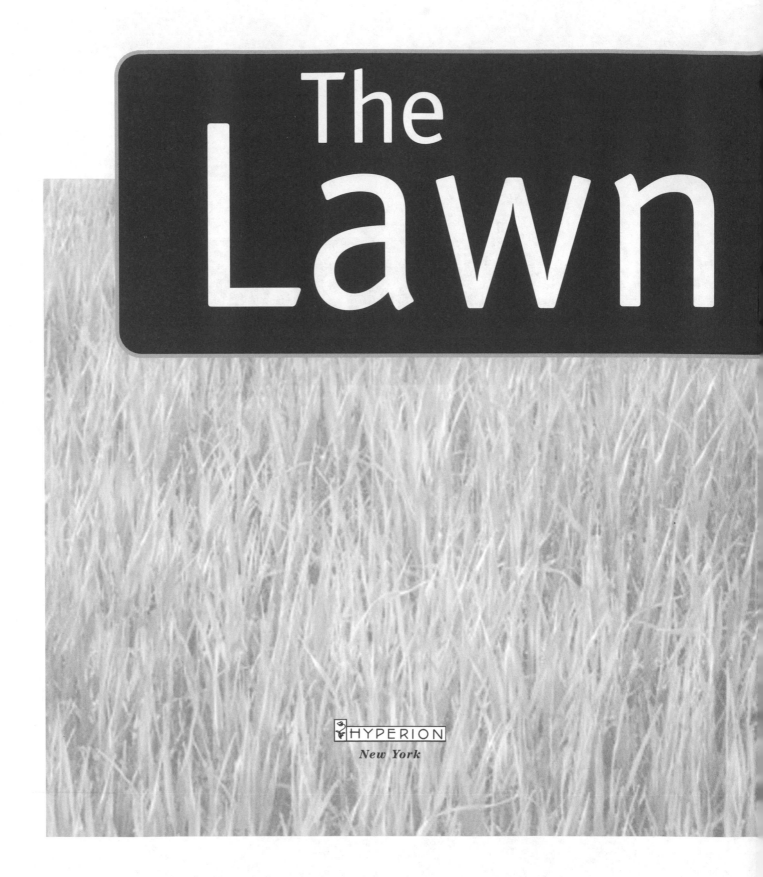

The
Lawn

HYPERION

New York

Bible

How to Keep It Green, Groomed, and Growing Every Season of the Year

DAVID R. MELLOR

A LARK PRODUCTION

Library of Congress Cataloging-in-Publication Data

   Mellor, David R.
      The lawn bible : how to keep it green, groomed, and growing every season
        of the year / David Mellor.
          p.   cm.
        ISBN 0-7868-8842-3
        1. Lawns.   I. Title
      SB433.M388   2003
      635.9'647–dc21   2002192174

Hyperion books are available for special promotions and premiums. For details contact Hyperion Special Markets, 77 West 66th Street, 11th floor, New York, New York, 10023, or call 212-456-0133.

Line illustrations by Elayne Sears
Stadium pattern photos by David Mellor
Book design by Lee Fukui

First Edition

10   9   8   7   6   5   4   3   2

To my magnificent wife, Denise, and
our loving daughters, Cacky and Tori, and
in loving memory of my brother Terry

ACKNOWLEDGMENTS

Denise, Cacky, and Tori—Your energy, humor, and love keep me going. Your smiles and hugs make my days complete. Thank you!

Mom, Chip, and Alison—Thank you for your guidance and support throughout the years. Your advice to find a career I loved so I wouldn't have to "go to work" each day has helped make my work life pleasurable and this project possible.

David and Paula Ann—Thank you for Denise, the values and work ethic she learned on the farm, and for always being there for us. She is an inspiration to me.

Karen Watts and the great team at Lark Productions—Thank you for your enthusiasm, support, help, and guidance through the writing of this book. You made it possible and fun. And to Rachel Hoyt, thanks for your tireless, swift, and enthusiastic editorial heroics.

George and Jeanne Garifallou—You were there for the beginning of this project. Your willingness to participate in late-night brainstorming and business planning sessions is really appreciated.

John Kramer—Your ideas and tireless energy for public relations are amazing. Thank you for all you do.

The Boston Red Sox—Thank you for the opportunity to work for the team I've loved all my life.

Skip DeWall—Thank you for your support and friendship through the years. They mean a lot to me.

My many friends and colleagues who contributed to *The Lawn Bible*—Thank you for your creativity and wisdom.

Hyperion—Thank you to Bob Miller and Mary Ellen O'Neill for your enthusiasm and energetic vision for this book.

CONTENTS

INTRODUCTION:
THE GOSPEL OF GRASS,
ACCORDING TO DAVE

Here's what I believe:

1. Great lawns are where memories are made. The feeling of a lush carpet of green under bare feet. The smell of freshly cut grass. A pileup of grass-stained kids in a rowdy neighborhood game of football. That first $5 you earned cutting someone else's lawn. It's up to you to create a lawn where the memories *want* to happen.

2. You don't get a second chance to make a first impression; your lawn *is* your first impression. Have a lawn and yard that speak honestly of who you are and what you care about.

3. Lawns are as simple or as complicated as you make them. When you figure out how invested in your lawn you really want to be, create a regimen and embrace it. Whatever you invest in your lawn in time and resources, you will get out of it a hundredfold.

4. There is no ideal lawn. There's your ideal and there's my ideal, and those ideals could be worlds apart. That's why the lawn is a perfect expression of American individuality.

5. You could have many worse habits than an obsession with your lawn. If anyone gives you the business over your love affair with your lawn, remind them it's better to be growing and mowing than, say, blowing the family savings on a weekend in Vegas.

I'm a lucky man. I know my job as director of grounds at Fenway Park is the next best thing to actually playing in the big leagues. I've groomed grass and fields from San Francisco's Candlestick Park to Milwaukee's County Stadium to Fenway, home of the Boston Red Sox and my current domain. I think you can safely say I spend every waking, working hour thinking about lawns. I plan and experiment; I manage and maintain; I work with (and against) the elements to keep the grounds in my care in perfect playing order. I do it for the teams, I do it for the fans—and I do it for myself and my family. Applying the same techniques at home, where my lawn is always a work in progress, I get the same pleasure and sense of accomplishment when I've finished a Saturday's grooming as I do when I look out over the field just before the game's first ball is tossed.

My challenges and opportunities as a professional groundskeeper are no different than yours as a home landscaper. This is why I'm sure that everything I have learned after 20 years perfecting my turf-care techniques is something you can learn, too, and with the same spectacular, satisfying results. So many people ask me "How can I make my lawn as nice as a professional field or golf course?" That's why I decided it was time to share the secrets of solid, professional quality lawn care in *The Lawn Bible*.

This book contains the ABCs of growing and maintaining a great lawn and is loaded with unexpected and entertaining nuggets of information and anecdote that I've collected over the many miles of grass I've managed. This is Turf 101, a rock-solid foundation in lawn care, including tips, tricks, and stories from my pals in the professional lawn and grounds biz, as well as experts in dirt, bugs, chemical controls, and more from all over the country.

You'll get the step-by-step on how grass grows; you'll get the dirt on dirt; you'll get a degree in Integrated Pest Management (That would be an IPMBA!); and you'll even get how to be a "lawn artist" by adding dazzling mowing patterns to your green canvas. The book takes a simple, troubleshooting-from-the-start approach, and you'll find plentiful resources at the back of the book, including contact information for companies and organizations that can help you just when you need it most.

After more than two decades on my hands and knees working the turf, I know for a fact that Mother Nature will throw a curve ball—in the form of extreme heat, humidity, disease, bugs, you name it—every time she gets a chance. *The Lawn Bible* will help you face the pitch with confidence. By the time we're done, you'll be able to work smarter, not harder, on your lawn—and you'll grow and mow like a pro.

Whether you just like to putter around the lawn a bit or manicure your lawn to perfection, the act of caring for your lawn—a living family of grass plants—is therapeutic and brings us all back to our agrarian roots. By tending to your yard's form and function, you're creating an environment that suits the needs of your family and lifestyle—and that can handle all of the wear and tear you, your pets, and a neighborhood ball game can dish out.

For those of you in the meadow-loving, anti-lawn contingent: this book isn't for you. This book is for the unabashed "lawnatics," those of us who love the strategy and execution of home lawn care. Those of us who care about the curb appeal of a well-kept lawn. Those of us who like good old-fashioned green as much as (if not more than) many of the other colors you can find in a lawn and garden. Those of us who spend $40 billion every year on our lawns and lawn care.

You don't have to have a big lawn or expensive equipment to play—and win—the lawn game. You set your own goals, however modest or elaborate, and apply the principles you will learn in *The Lawn Bible*. There's no reason in the world you can't achieve a professional-looking lawn, as groomed and weedfree as the field at Fenway or as verdant and poetic as the Old Course at St. Andrew's in Scotland. *The Lawn Bible* will get you where you want to go.

David Mellor

GOOD GRASS, UP CLOSE

1

The Anatomy of a Blade of Grass

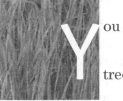ou know that old saying—you can't see the forest for the trees? Well, you can't see the lawn for the grass. That silky green carpet of lawn doesn't happen with just one plant. Lawns may be made up of millions of grass plants. Just think—if there are an average of six grass plants to a square inch of lawn, a 4,000-square-foot lawn has over 3 million plants. It's a little daunting to think of it that way—who wants to be in charge of 3 million plants? But looking at one of these plants up close is probably the best way to really begin to understand what goes on when you grow, mow, and care for your grass. When was the last time *you* got on your hands and knees and took a look at a grass plant?

The anatomy of grass can be broken down into three simple parts: what's above the ground, what's at ground level, and what's below the ground.

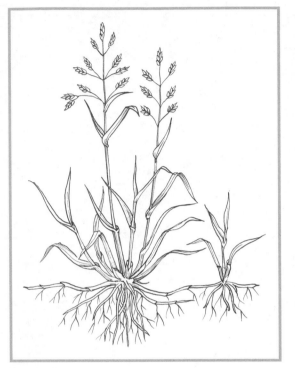

Grass Plant

Above the ground:

Shoot—anything above the ground is called a shoot.

Stem—supports the leaves of the plant.

Blade—the upper broad portion of the leaf.

Sheath—the rounded part at the base of the blade that wraps around the stem.

Collar—the point where the blade and sheath meet.

Nodes—swollen areas on the stem where the "buds" develop into new leafy tops when the grass is cut.

Tiller—secondary shoots that grow from the crown on the same grass plant.

Stolon—"runners" from the crown that create secondary shoots next to the original plant forming "daughter" plants.

Ground level:

Crown—the center of the plants' activity. The leaves and the roots originate from the crown.

Below the ground:

Roots—the network of anchors that keep the plant firmly in the ground. They soak up the food and water from the soil that the plant needs to live.

A Short History of the Lawn

The modern notion of a lawn in America—a nice, even blanket of green—has only been around for about 200 years. Before the nineteenth century, yards consisted of flower or vegetable gardens, trees, shrubs, and dirt. Trends in yards and gardens of Victorian England really sparked the interest in turfgrass in the United States. Wealthy English homeowners had sweeping lawns of green—and the requisite load of groundskeepers to keep them in shape. Many Americans who traveled to England during this time returned to the United States with dreamy images of creating these grand lawns. The problem was, any grass seed they brought back didn't survive stateside—thus the beginning of the search for our very own turfgrass.

Gathering grass seeds from all over the world, the U.S. Department of Agriculture began developing grasses that would produce those fine lawns in our country. While this was certainly a giant leap for the American lawn, the problem was taking care of them. The only way to cut grass at that time was by using a scythe, which was enormously time- and labor-intensive. Alternatively, one could let animals graze on the grass and chew it short. With the invention of a reel-type mower in 1830 (thank you, Edwin Budding), the problem of grass cutting was to become a thing of the past. Americans, always game for a new gadget, took immediately to the lawn mower, and soon English-scale lawns began sprouting up all over the United States, and, today, we are a proud, green land.

Rhizomes—an underground stem that travels from the original plant to grow into a secondary shoot to create a "daughter" plant.

What Makes Grass a Lawn

The lawn surface that stands up to modern life—sports, parks, rough ground cover, landscaping, and children—can't be just any grass. Corn. Wheat. Sugarcane. These are all species of grass, but you wouldn't want them for a lawn. Out of the over 10,000 species of grass, only about 50 species can produce a lawn.

Turfgrass—that's what makes grass a lawn. Turfgrasses are species of grass that are smaller and more compact, can be mowed, and actually benefit from mowing. They are lower growing and thus more dense at mowing height—giving them the ability to recover after the cut. Turfgrasses are meant to grow crowded together, which is how the tightly knit carpet of green lawn is made. This grouping of grasses also helps the lawn resist wear and tear from the people who grow them.

Types of Grasses

The goal of anyone planting a lawn is survival of the grass, right? Choosing the right type of grass to grow will save you time, money, and heartache. Whether you're starting a lawn from scratch or trying to improve the lawn you've got, the right choice of grass is imperative. Why spend hours preparing, planting, and tending to your grass either to fight with it year after year or to watch it wither and die altogether because of a bad choice of grass.

The easiest way to distinguish the best grass to grow in your yard is by your climate. Grass species are separated into two categories of growth areas—cool season and warm season. This distinction is based on what grass will survive in any given area and how the grass grows (or not) throughout the year. It will also determine when your lawn needs to be tended to and how much work you can expect to do.

Cool season grasses simply are more adaptable in the northern regions with shorter summers and colder winters. They grow vigorously during the cool spring and fall at temperatures between 60° and 70° F. This is the time when they need the most mowing and feeding. In the summer, these grasses grow more slowly and may go dormant in heat and drought. Cooler weather and proper watering will bring them back to their former splendor. In areas where the ground freezes during the winter, cool season grasses will go dormant and recover in the spring thaw.

Warm season grasses thrive in the southern regions, where summers are long and hot and winters are mild. These grasses grow most actively during the warm summer months. They aren't as cold hardy as cool season grasses and may go dormant and turn brown during the cooler winter months or even die off altogether in temperatures that are unusually cold. Warm season grasses are robust —often growing in less than desirable soils and clay. They are often overseeded with cool season grasses in the fall to provide a green lawn year round.

The problem with this division of grasses is that not everyone lives in a climate that is strictly either warm or cold. In fact, there's a good-sized belt across the midsection of the country that falls into what's called the " transition zone" between warm season grass and cool season grass regions. In transition areas, such as Oklahoma, West Virginia, and Kentucky, the winters are too cool for the warm season grasses and the summers are too hot for the cool season grasses, which can present a dilemma for the home lawn grower. If you live in one of these iffy areas, be sure to check with your local agricultural extension office or a reputable local nursery for information regarding which grasses will grow best in your area. The best grass varieties to use are ones that have higher extremes in either the cool or warm tolerance range. Cool season grasses that have a higher tolerance to heat and warm season grasses that have a higher tolerance to cold are your best bet. Keep in mind that even with a good seed mix, lawns in the transitional zone may need more effort to keep them beautiful throughout the seasons.

When looking over the following descriptions of grass types, also keep in mind the kind of use your lawn will have to withstand. Are you going to have a showcase lawn? A kid-friendly lawn with a swing set or a pitchback? Volleyball games every other weekend?

Choosing the right grass is all about determining its suitability not only for your climate, but also for your lifestyle.

Expert Advice

You will find that your best allies in the which-grass-is-best-for-me dialogue are the local experts—specifically your local agricultural extension office. These folks are a terrific resource for all kinds of local horticultural information, including which kind of grass grows best in your area. They're also good for the scoop on soil testing, pest identification and control, and even classification of lawn diseases. For the extension office nearest you, consult the blue government pages in your local phone book under county or state government.

Tricks of the Trade: Seed Scoop

Because of what I do for a living, I'm particular about my seed. For the field at Fenway as well as for my own home lawn, I order custom blended seed mixes from my professional suppliers—but not before checking with my friends at the National Turfgrass Evaluation Program (NTEP) to determine that year's best-rated turfgrass species for my area. NTEP is the best source for seasonal info on what's growing well where, as well as which new cultivars have been introduced in various regions around the country. After I've gotten the latest update from NTEP, I order my seed. Go to *www.ntep.org* for access to the information that no turfgrass professional could do without.

The truth is, you get exactly what you pay for with grass seed, so if you try to look for bargains, you're likely to end up with dirty, weedy seed. My favorite commercially available seed brand is Scott's. It's always clean, weed-free, cropseed-free seed. And worth whatever you have to pay for it.

David Mellor

Cool Season Grasses

These grass varieties will grow well in the northern regions of the country, as well as in cooler coastal regions where the temperatures don't exceed 90° F for long periods of time. Some of them are also used to overseed warm season lawns, to keep a green lawn year round.

KENTUCKY BLUEGRASS *(Poa pratensis)*

A lawn of Kentucky bluegrass is often considered the lawn by which all other lawns are judged. Characterized by the deep green/blue color and the fine texture, Kentucky bluegrass is as durable as it is good looking. It is exceptionally tolerant to the cold and it recovers quickly from cutting or abuse. It is also very drought resistant—going dormant during the dry weather, it quickly regains its color and vitality when sufficient water is available.

Uses

Lawns, parks, golf fairways, athletic fields, anywhere a dense turf is desired.

Advantages

Kentucky bluegrass is desirable as a turfgrass because it recuperates well after drought, use, and mowing. When mowed at higher levels (2½ to 3 inches) it hinders weeds from forming. It has good weed tolerance, grows well in colder climates, and it forms a dense turf.

Disadvantages

Kentucky bluegrass has poor shade tolerance in the northeast quadrant of the country. In the southern regions, it needs a little shade to get through the hot summer months. It requires more frequent watering and fertilizing than other types of grass to maintain the deep green color. It sprouts slowly when planted, especially in cool weather.

Maintenance Level
Moderate to high, although new varieties require less watering and fertilization.

Propagation
Rhizomes and tillers.

When to Plant
Fall, spring.

Some Varieties
Adelphi, Blacksburg, Eclipse, Glade, Midnight, Merion, Touchdown.

CHEWING FESCUE *(Festuca rubra communtata)*

This aggressive, fine-textured grass can tolerate poor, acidic soils. It is also shade, cold, and drought resistant. It is commonly used in mixtures with other cool-season turfgrasses (such as Kentucky bluegrass) for use on low-maintenance or somewhat shady lawns.

Uses
Low-maintenance areas and low-traffic areas in lawns and parks.

Advantages
Well adapted to sandy, acidic, and low-moisture soils. Very shade tolerant.

Disadvantages
Aggressive, so may overtake other turfgrasses. Does not stand up well to heavy traffic and is slow to recover from damage. May develop thatch easily in acidic soils.

Maintenance Level
Low to moderate.

Propagation
Seed.

When to Plant
Fall, spring.

Some Varieties
Banner, Jamestown, Waldorf.

PERENNIAL RYEGRASS *(Lolium perenne)*

Perennial ryegrass is often combined in seed mixes with Kentucky bluegrass because it establishes quickly, filling in the lawn while the bluegrass takes longer to grow. It has fine-textured, shiny blades that are deep green. It is often used in high traffic areas and well-used lawns as it stands up very well to wear.

Uses
Lawns, playing fields, overseeding warm-season grasses to produce color during the winter.

Advantages
Very wear tolerant. Germinates quickly and grows swiftly—often showing shoots in only three days. Does not require much water or fertilizer.

Disadvantages
Not as cold tolerant as Kentucky bluegrass. As a bunchgrass, perennial ryegrass does easily fill in damaged areas. Prone to blade shredding.

Maintenance Level
Low to moderate.

Propagation
Seed.

When to Plant
Fall, spring; fall when used to winter overseed warm season grasses.

Some Varieties
Citation II, Manhattan II, SR-4200.

TALL FESCUE *(Festuca arundinacea)*

Tall fescue was once considered a pasture grass. New turf-type varieties are finer in texture with a lower growth pattern that produces a good, rich colored lawn.

Uses
Lawns, playgrounds, athletic fields, rough acreage, and along roads.

Advantages
Tall fescue has a high shade, heat, and drought tolerance. It prefers high mowing and survives well without much fertilization. It also stands up very well to wear.

Disadvantages
Can be clumpy in appearance, especially in older varieties. Most tall fescues don't mix well with other grasses. Although better cultivated, most tall fescues are coarser than other types of turfgrass.

Maintenance Level
Low.

Propagation
Primarily tillers, although some varieties may have short rhizomes.

When to Plant
Fall, spring.

Some Varieties
Amigo, Apache, Rebel, Tribute, Wrangler.

RED FESCUE *(Festuca rubra)*

Red fescue (aka creeping red fescue) is often combined with Kentucky bluegrass in fine quality seed mixes. With its fine-textured, deep green leaves, it often grows well where Kentucky bluegrass doesn't—in shady and drought-prone areas.

Uses

Well adapted to shady areas, banks, and slopes. Red fescue is also good for overseeding dormant warm-weather grasses, as long as the area is low traffic.

Advantages

Shade tolerant and drought tolerant, it also grows well in acidic soil. Sprouts quickly.

Disadvantages

Red fescue does not tolerate wet soils or clay and is less heat tolerant than other fescues. Does not stand up well to heavy wear. Spreads slowly.

Maintenance Level

Low to moderate.

Propagation

Short rhizomes.

When to Plant

Fall, spring; fall when used to winter overseed warm season grasses.

Some Varieties

Ensylvia, Flyer, Pennlawn, Ruby.

ROUGH BLUEGRASS *(Poa trivialis)*

The attractive, light green rough bluegrass isn't as highbrow as its Kentucky cousin, but it will grow where Kentucky bluegrass won't—in shady and moist areas. It is cold tolerant but wears poorly.

Uses

Lawns (if well watered and fertilized) and shaded parts of golf courses.

Advantages

Shade tolerant and winter hardy. Tolerates lower mowing heights. Establishes well from seed and is fast sprouting.

Disadvantages

Does not grow well in full sun. Recovers slowly from wear because of its weak and shallow roots. In most places, it requires irrigation.

Maintenance Level

Moderate to high.

Propagation

Stolons.

When to Plant

Fall, spring; fall when used to winter overseed warm season grasses.

Some Varieties

Colt, Cypress, Dark Horse, Snowbird.

CANADA BLUEGRASS *(Poa compress)*

Uses

Low-maintenance areas, banks, low traffic areas, and hard-to-access areas.

Advantages

Can survive in very poor soil. Has some shade tolerance.

Disadvantages

Doesn't recover well from wear. It has sparse turf—not thick and dense like the Kentucky bluegrass.

Maintenance Level
Low.

Propagation
Short rhizomes.

When to Plant
Fall, spring.

Some Varieties
Canon, Reubens.

ANNUAL BLUEGRASS *(Poa annua)*

This is a weed grass that has no practical application in lawn use. Stay away from seed mixes that contain it.

HARD FESCUE *(Festuca longifolia)*

Hard fescue is a fine-textured, slow-growing grass that requires limited maintenance. Its short and slow growth needs less frequent mowing. It mixes well with ryes and bluegrasses.

Uses
Low-maintenance areas, slopes, and banks.

Advantages
The most heat tolerant of the fescues, it grows well in shady and drought-prone areas. Requires less frequent mowing and needs minimum maintenance when mature.

Disadvantages
Not very wear-resistant, the hard fescue grows slowly and has a shallow root system.

Maintenance Level
Low.

Propagation
Tillers.

When to Plant
Fall, spring.

Some Varieties
Biljart, Reliant, Waldina.

CREEPING BENTGRASS *(Agrostis palustris)*

Creeping bentgrass is the finest texture, lowest growing of all the grasses. It is soft, dense, and creates a lovely carpetlike turf. It is usually out of the realm of lawn turf for homeowners due to the high maintenance requirements.

Uses
Creeping bentgrass is perfect for putting greens, lawn bowling greens, and tennis courts.

Advantages
It tolerates very low mowing (¼ inch) and recovers well from damage.

Disadvantages
High-maintenance. Requires frequent mowing to keep it short. If allowed to grow over an inch, the blades tend to bend (hence, the name) in a sideways growth pattern instead of upright. It requires frequent watering during the summer (at least twice a week), good drainage, and repeated fertilization. Prone to thatch.

Maintenance Level
High.

Propagation
Stolons.

Top Ten Lawns

While all turf grasses have their advantages and disadvantages, here are the most popular grass choices for lawns and their best features.

Cool Season

1. Kentucky Bluegrass—beautiful color and recovers well from damage.

2. Fine Fescue—requires lower maintenance, some shade tolerance, and many varieties are cultivated with insect resistant endophytes.

3. Perennial Ryegrass—establishes quickly and is very wear tolerant.

4. Tall Fescue—heat, shade, and drought resistant and tolerates wear well.

5. Red Fescue—shade and drought tolerant.

Warm Season

1. Bermuda Grass—drought and cold tolerant, fills in fast, and is commonly disease free.

2. St. Augustine Grass—tough, fast growing with deep roots.

3. Buffalo Grass—drought tolerant, and generally low maintenance.

4. Zoysia Grass—attractive, wear tolerant, and drought resistant.

5. Bahiagrass—grows very well in sandy or acidic soil.

When to Plant

Fall, spring.

Some Varieties

Lopez, Penncross, Southshore.

REDTOP (*Agrostis alba*)

Redtop bentgrass has no practical application in lawns. It is used mainly for ground cover along roadways and in ditches.

ANNUAL RYEGRASS *(Lolium multiforum)*

Annual ryegrass is not heat, shade, drought, or cold tolerant. It lives for only one season and may be used for a temporary lawn or for winter overseeding a southern grass to keep the color in the winter. Stay away from cheap seed mixes that contain annual ryegrass—you'll be wasting your time and your money as it will die out, leaving a patchy and sparse lawn.

Warm Season Grasses

These grass varieties thrive in the heat of southern climates. They can also grow in the southern areas of cooler climates, provided the ground doesn't freeze.

BERMUDA GRASS *(Cynodon* species*)*

Bermuda grass is as popular for lawns in the south as Kentucky bluegrass is in the north. A good low-maintenance lawn, the coarse-textured Bermuda grass grows well in poor soil and tolerates low mowing. It is salt tolerant and has deep roots, which makes it drought and heat tolerant. Bermuda grass is sensitive to the cold. At temperatures below 50° to 60° F, it will often go dormant and turn brown.

Uses

Lawns (especially high-traffic areas), athletic fields, golf courses, school grounds, parks.

Advantages

Fast growing and dense—able to fill in areas quickly. Tolerates low mowing and is salt tolerant. Bermuda grass survives drought by going into dormancy and easily comes back to life with adequate water. Very tolerant of wear.

Disadvantages

Cool temperatures can easily kill Bermuda grass. It does not tolerate shade. Hybrids may need more care than common types and must be started by springs or plugs. Aggressive common Bermuda grass may invade areas outside the lawn—i.e., gardens and walk-ways.

Maintenance Level

Average (common Bermuda grass) to high (certain hybrid types).

Propagation

Seed (common Bermuda grass) or sprigs and plugs (hybrids—which are sterile).

When to Plant

Early summer.

Some Varieties

Sundevil, Yuma (common) and NuMex Sahara, Tifgreen, Tifway (hybrid).

ST. AUGUSTINE GRASS

(Stenotaphrum scundatum)

St. Augustine grass is medium- to coarse-textured grass that forms a thick, dense turf that squeezes out all other grasses. It is the most shade tolerant of all the warm season grasses. It requires frequent mowing in the height of the summer and should be mowed to a height of 2 to 4 inches to deter weeds and thatch.

Uses

Lawns, golf course roughs.

Advantages

Shade tolerant and stays green longer during heat stress.

Disadvantages

Not at all cold tolerant. Frequent mowing, watering, and fertilization are required during peak growing season. Doesn't produce a partic-ularly elegant lawn, even with proper care.

Maintenance Level

High.

Propagation

Extensive network of stolons.

When to Plant

Early summer.

Some Varieties

DelMar, Floratam, Floratine, Seville.

BUFFALO GRASS *(Buchloe dactyloides)*

Buffalo grass, another of the native grasses used for turfgrass, is a fine textured, hardy grass. It is extremely heat tolerant and can be left to grow without mowing (8 to 10 inches), but will appear more turflike with mowing to 3 to 4 inches. It can grow in areas that receive only 10 to 15 inches of rainfall a year, but does well with some watering.

Uses

Low-use areas, lawns.

Advantages

High heat tolerance. Requires little, if any, mowing.

Disadvantages

Will brown quickly in midsummer. Does not tolerate shade. Seed is expensive.

Maintenance Level

Low.

Propagation

Stolons and seed.

When to Plant

Early summer.

Some Varieties

609, Prairie, Texoka.

ZOYSIA GRASS *(Zoysia* species*)*

Zoysia grass is often touted in magazine advertisements as a " miracle grass." While its thick dense turf is drought resistant and can withstand wear well, it is extremely slow growing—it often takes two to three seasons to properly fill in. Once filled in, however, it forms a beautiful, if a little prickly, lawn.

Uses

Lawns, golf courses.

Advantages

Drought resistant and requires less mowing than other warm season grasses.

Disadvantages

Very slow growing and is usually established by plugs that may take two to three years to become fully established. Browns early in the fall and is slow to recover in the spring. Will take moderate wear, but not for areas that take constant abuse (such as playing fields). The coarse texture of the stiff blades makes for a bristly lawn that may be too rough for bare feet.

Maintenance Level

Moderate.

Propagation

Rhizomes and stolons.

When to Plant

Early summer.

Some Varieties

El Toro, Emerald, Meyer.

BAHIAGRASS *(Paspalum notatum)*

Bahiagrass is a coarse, rugged grass that has come a long way. Once used mainly for low-maintenance areas such as roadsides, it has become an inexpensive way to grow a lawn in the south. An aggressive grass, it can choke out weeds, as well as other grass varieties. It is shade tolerant. Bahiagrass has an extensive root system that will help keep it alive in sandy conditions. It will pull every bit of water that it can from the soil, reducing the need for irrigation. The root system also makes it ideal for erosion-prone areas.

Uses

Lawns, golf courses, and roadsides.

Advantages

Salt and shade tolerant. Tough blades, making for excellent durability.

Disadvantages

The tough blades require frequent mowing with a sharp blade to keep the lawn looking good. Reel mowers are not recommended.

Maintenance Level

Low to moderate due to the need for frequent mowing.

Propagation

Short rhizomes.

When to Plant

Early summer.

Some Varieties

Argentine, Paraguay, Pensacola.

CENTIPEDE GRASS *(Eremochloa ophiuroides)*

Centipede grass is a good low-maintenance choice for a lawn that's more for looks than for down and dirty use. It is slow growing with a shallow root system, making it unsuitable for high-traffic areas with a low drought tolerance. It reaches a mature height of only 3 to 4 inches. It requires less mowing than other warm season grasses.

Uses

Lawns, golf courses.

Advantages

Low maintenance and easy to establish. Grows well in poor and acidic soils.

Disadvantages

Requires frequent irrigation, especially during drought conditions. Does not tolerate the cold and may not recover at all after a few frosts. Will not tolerate salt spray.

Maintenance Level

Low.

Propagation

Stolons.

When to Plant

Early summer.

Some Varieties

Centennial, Oaklawn, Tiblair.

BLUE GRAMA GRASS *(Bouteloua gracilis)*

Blue Grama grass is a native grass of the Great Plains. It is one of a few native grasses grown as turfgrass in North America. It tolerates drought and both heat and cold.

Uses

Lawns, roadsides, and conservation areas.

Advantages

Can withstand cold fluctuations to −40° F, but may go dormant. Requires mowing only three to four times a year to maintain a turflike look.

Disadvantages

Sparse, open turf. May go dormant and turn brown in extreme cold temperatures.

Maintenance Level

Low.

Propagation

Short rhizomes.

When to Plant

Early summer.

Some Varieties

Only the species is available. No cultivars have been developed.

Best Grass Combos

How do you choose grass seed when your yard has less than optimal conditions? That shady area under the elm tree hardly gets any sun, yet the front yard is in full sun all day? Do you expect a yard full of children running around all summer? Think

Overseeding Warm Season Grasses

Grass owners in the southern climates and the southwest have a unique opportunity—they can keep their grass green all year long. No, there's no miracle grass that will last through all the seasons. There *is* a way to use different types of grass during the year to take advantage of the growing times while the seasons change.

Warm season grasses often go dormant and turn brown during the winter. This is the perfect time to cover up that brown grass by overseeding with a more cold-tolerant cool season grass. When the weather heats up in the spring, the cool season grass will die off and the warm season grass will green up and continue the green lawn.

Not all cool season grasses are suitable to use for overseeding in the winter. The grass must germinate quickly in the fall and then die out in the spring to allow the warm season grass to recover. Perennial ryegrass, rough bluegrass, and red fescue are the most popular choices of grass for winter overseeding.

about how you want your lawn to be used, what climate you're in, the conditions in your yard, and how much time you want to spend working on your lawn. Once you've got that figured out, you're ready to take a look at the grass seed you're likely to use for your lawn.

First, a little bit of vocabulary relating to grass seed:

Blend—Seed packages that are sold with a combination of two or more varieties of one species of grass. A Kentucky bluegrass blend may contain Adelphi and Merion varieties of Kentucky bluegrass.

Mix—Seed packages that are made up of two or more different grass species. A cool season mix may contain a combination of Kentucky bluegrass and fescue with a splash of perennial ryegrass added.

Tricks of the Trade: Snakes and Warm Season Grasses

One of the challenges we encounter here at Qualcomm Stadium is preventing the baseball from zigzagging across the grass on its way to the outfielders. This is commonly referred to in baseball terms as "snaking" and is created by improper mowing. When mowing the same grass area in the same direction each time, grass blades have a tendency to lay down in the direction the mower travels. This creates "grain" as it's known in agronomic terms and is more prevalent with closely mowed warm season grasses, particularly hybrid Bermuda. There are few things worse for a professional baseball groundskeeper than to have an outfielder running toward a speeding grounder, reaching down with his glove to field the ball in an effort to throw out the runner who is attempting to stretch a single into a double, only to have the ball snake. I'll never forget the time when this happened to the Padres right fielder, Tony Gywnn. After the ball scooted by his glove, he had to stop quickly to go back to retrieve it, and any attempt at throwing out the runner was lost. With the runner now standing on second base when Tony fired the ball to the infield, I was praying the runner wouldn't score. When the inning was over, Tony came looking for me in the ground-crew area next to the Padres dugout and we had a quick discussion. He did most of the talking and when he was finished I was left with a very clear picture of my next day's work . . . remove the snake!

With warm season grasses that prefer closer mowing heights, alternating mowing directions and frequent vertical mowing (verticutting) are common practices to minimize the grain (snake).

Steve Wightman
Stadium Turf Manager
Qualcomm Stadium
San Diego, California

These blends and mixes are more commonly sold than single grasses. They are combined to make a good-looking, adaptable lawn. For example, where one grass in a mix may not be able to make it in the shade, another will, so your lawn survives in a variety of conditions in your yard.

The following is a quick glance at types of grass for your location or for your specific yard condition. Remember, it's a good idea to check with your local extension office to find out what grasses grow best in your area.

The United States can be divided into five different climatic zones for turfgrass. In each of these regions, certain grasses will thrive while others won't.

Zone 1: Cool, Humid

Cool season grasses grow well all around this area, but may go dormant during a summer with little rainfall. In the interior of the region, buffalo grass can be grown. In the southern part of the area and on the Atlantic coast, you can grow zoysia grass.

Zone 2: Cool, Arid

Cool season grasses grow in this zone, but will need irrigation. Buffalo grass will grow in the interior portion.

Zone 3: Warm, Arid

Warm season grasses grow in this area, with Bermuda grass being the most prevalent.

These grasses may need irrigation to grow well. In the northern region of the zone, buffalo grass will grow.

Zone 4: Warm, Humid

As in Zone 3, warm season grasses are the rule. Plant zoysia grass in the northern area, St. Augustine, centipede, and bahia grass along the coast, and Bermuda grass pretty much anywhere in the region.

> **CHAPTER & VERSE**
>
> Different conditions in your yard require different types of seed. First determine your climatic area, then determine the trouble spots in your yard, such as shady areas or high traffic areas. Look for seed blends that have grass to cover the variety of situations in your yard.

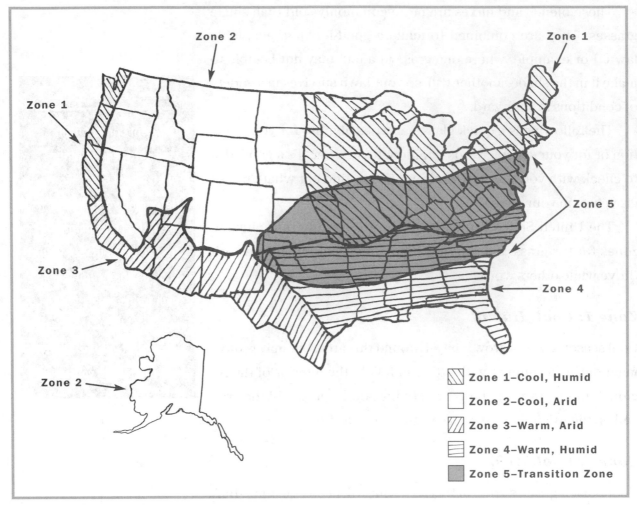

Zone 2

Zone 1

Zone 1

Zone 5

Zone 3

Zone 4

Zone 2

Zone 1–Cool, Humid
Zone 2–Cool, Arid
Zone 3–Warm, Arid
Zone 4–Warm, Humid
Zone 5–Transition Zone

*United States Climate Regions
for Turfgrass*

Zone 5: Transition Zone

This is the most difficult area to choose turfgrass for planting. It encompasses different parts of all four zones, so choosing a grass is tricky. Neither the warm season nor the cool season grass is appropriate across the entire zone. Choose grasses that have the most tolerance to heat, cold, and drought from the warm or cool season types. In this zone, it is best to check with your local extension office for help in determining what grass will grow in your particular area.

The following lists show the types of grasses you can choose to grow according to the available sun and shade in your yard.

Shade

Rough bluegrass—cool season

Chewings fescue—cool season

Tall fescue—cool season

St. Augustine grass—warm season

Centipede grass—warm season

Bahiagrass—warm season

Zoysia grass—warm season

Sun

Kentucky bluegrass—cool season

Fine fescue—cool season

Bermuda grass—warm season

Buffalo grass—warm season

Bits of Both Sun and Shade

Kentucky bluegrass, fine fescue, and perennial ryegrass—
cool season

Bermuda grass, centipede grass, and zoysia grass—
warm season

Starting with Seed

Where to Buy

Buy your grass seed from a reputable source such as a lawn and garden center or home improvement retailer. Buy the best seed available and expect to pay some money for quality grass seed. After all, there's a reason that the cheap seed is cheap. Shop early in the season for your grass seed so you can get the best selection of fresh seed instead of the end-of-the-season dregs. If you're buying seed from a catalog or online, be sure the company is dependable and keep all correspondence in case you have problems with the product. Many national brands of grass seed carry a guarantee for their

Seed Package Label

products. Keep your receipt and a copy of the guarantee so if you're not happy with the results you can write them a note and perhaps get some of your money back.

What to Look For

You walk into the store and are faced with all of these seed packages. Pictures of beautiful lawns and words like "miracle lawn" and "fast growing" scream out at you. While the pictures might be pretty and the words sound good, it's what's inside the package that you want to investigate.

Deciphering a seed package is as simple as reading the label on a can of soup. You've already become familiar with the grasses that will survive in your area, so you're already one step ahead in the seed game. The Federal Seed Act of 1936 mandated more detailed and uniform labeling on all seed packaging in the United States. So, the information you find on a seed package in Rhode Island is the same as the information you find on a seed package in California. Reading the label is easy—you just need to know what all that information means and how it relates to your lawn.

Kind and Variety. This part of the seed package lists the particular grass seed it contains—both the type and variety of grass. Look for grasses with specific variety names, such as "Merion Kentucky Bluegrass," instead of the generic "Kentucky Bluegrass." The generic seed may contain common types of the grass that usually don't have the same desirable characteristics of the specific cultivars. Cheaper grass seeds will usually contain the generic types of grass.

Germination Percentage. This number represents the percentage of grass seeds you can expect to germinate in optimum conditions. Don't buy seeds with germination percentages less than 70 %.

Pure Seed Percentages. The percentage of seeds contained in the package by weight, not count.

Inert Matter. This is the amount of stuff in the package that won't grow—such as chaff and dirt—that gets caught up in the production process. This number should be less than 1% and even zero in good seed mixes.

Other Crop Seeds. These are other commercially grown grass crop seeds—such as orchardgrass or timothy grass—that may be contained in the package. As these crops are not desirable in a lawn, this number should be zero or as close to zero as possible.

Weed Seed. Almost all grass seed packages have at least some weed seed since it is nearly impossible to keep out. Look for less than 1% of weed seed.

Noxious Weed Seed. Some weeds have been declared noxious in most states. Buy seed that has no noxious weed seed at all.

Origin. The place where the seed crop was grown.

Date. This is the date the seed was tested. Often a "sell by" date will also be listed. Look for dates in the current year.

Lot Number and Manufacturer Information. A seed package must have a lot number to ensure the contents listed are indeed what's in the package. The manufacturer's name and address must also be listed on the package.

One last bit of advice about the package label. Unless you're looking for a temporary lawn, avoid packages containing annual ryegrass. This grass will die out in one season, leaving patchy spots in the lawn that you'll have to reseed the next year.

CHAPTER & VERSE

Buy the freshest seed available and shop early for the best selection. Don't buy last year's seed—you risk the chance of lower seed germination the longer the seed is on the shelf.

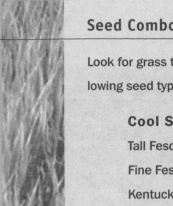

Seed Combos for Tough, Kid-Proof Lawns

Look for grass types that have higher wear tolerance. Mixtures of these following seed types hold up best to kid traffic.

Cool Season Grasses	Warm Season Grasses
Tall Fescue	Zoysia Grass
Fine Fescue	Bermuda Grass
Kentucky Bluegrass	Bahia Grass

If you really love your lawn, get to know your grass, starting with the seed. With all the different kinds of grass out there, you can tailor your choice to *your* needs, when you're armed with the right information. Figure out how you want to use your lawn, what you want it to look like, how much time you want to spend tending it, and then choose the grass that's right for you. A smart pick from the start just makes good lawn sense.

THE HEART AND START OF A GREAT NEW LAWN: THE SOIL

2

S tarting a new lawn from scratch gives you the best chance to have a great lawn. Whether you've just purchased a new home and you're looking at a dirt yard or you've gotten rid of a really bad lawn and you're ready to start over, there's one thing you can't overlook—the soil.

Start with the Test

Why do you need to test your soil? Let's see. If saving time, money, and aggravation are important to you, have the soil tested. If not, go ahead and wing it—with your fingers crossed and your wallet open. A soil test is the easiest way to find out what your soil has andwhat it doesn't. A soil test will determine the levels of pH, phosphorous, potassium, and organic matter in your soil, as well as the percentage of sand, silt, and clay. If any one of these factors is off, you can easily correct it prior to planting the grass. This will give you a healthier, more disease-resistant lawn that will be less work—and less expensive—in the long run.

Your local agricultural extension office or a nearby university can usually perform a professional soil test for a very modest fee. If not, there are private labs that provide the same service, but with a higher price tag. Look for a private lab in your local Yellow Pages under "Soil—Analysis," "Soil—Testing," or "Laboratories—Testing." The results will come back in two to four weeks with information about your soil, recommendations as to what your soil needs, and what specific amounts of lime, sulfur, fertilizer, or organic matter to add. For a nominal cost (compared to perhaps years of future problems), you'll end up with a good soil base with which to start your lawn.

There are home soil-test kits available at garden centers and nurseries, but they'll only be able to tell you what the pH of your lawn is. You really want to know more than just the pH to make sure your soil is as good as it can be, so laying out a few bucks for a professional test is really your best bet.

Now, how do you go about getting the soil sample for the test? Easy. Follow these steps and you'll be sending out a good, representative soil sample for analysis.

1. Plan to send off the soil sample three to four weeks before you plan to plant your grass. This allows enough time for the results to come back so you can make any necessary corrections to the pH or nutrient deficiency in the soil before you plant.

2. Be sure you have clean tools. A rusty or fertilizer-encrusted tool or bucket can easily contaminate your soil sample. Clean all tools and buckets thoroughly or start with new ones. If you clean them, be sure to rinse them well so no soapy residue remains to foul the sample. You'll need a clean core sampler, a clean trowel or shovel, and a clean container to hold the soil.

3. Using the core sampler, trowel, or shovel, take a cut of the soil. Be sure to get soil to a depth of at least 6 inches deep for the sample. If using a trowel or shovel, take a thin slice of soil, not a whole shovel or trowelfull (you don't need much).

4. Continue taking samples from eight to ten different areas around your yard. Get at least two samples from every 1,000 square feet of lawn space. Remove as much grass as possible from the soil. Go ahead and throw all the samples in the same container because you're going to mix them all up together anyway.

5. Thoroughly mix the soil from all the samples. Take a cup or two of soil out of this mixture and place it into the container provided by the soil lab.

6. If you have any areas of particular concern in your yard, such as areas where the grass won't grow well or new seeds won't take, send in a separate sample for analysis on those particular areas. If you have an exceptionally large planting area, you may want to take separate samples, say from the front and the backyards, for separate analysis. Most often for yards of average size and layout, one sample per yard is enough.

> **CHAPTER & VERSE**
>
> Make sure you get a good representative sample of the soil in your yard. Take the time to follow the instructions for getting a clean sample. The soil test results will only be as good as the soil sample itself.

That's it. When you get the results back, the lab will have calculated the levels of the specific nutrients in your soil and the pH and give you recommendations about what types and how much of each nutrient you need to add to your soil for optimum grass growth.

The Test Results

You should get the results in two to four weeks, delivered either by snail mail or email. You've got the results in your hand, but how do you read them? Here is a breakdown of what you'll see to help you interpret your test.

pH—the pH level of your soil is indicated. A pH level of between 6.7 and 7.3 means your soil is neutral, a pH level of less than 6.7 means you soil is acidic, and a level greater than 7.3 means your soil is alkaline.

Available nutrients and micronutrients—measures of nitrogen, phosphorus, potassium, calcium, and magnesium available in the soil.

Soluble salts—a measure of the salt level in the soil.

Organic matter—indicates the fertility of the soil.

CEC—a measure of the soil's ability to hold nutrients.

Recommendations—a list of the particular amendments and what amounts you should add to your soil for peak performance.

Use this soil report now, as you prepare to seed your lawn. You'll also use it if you're renovating your lawn later, so hang on to it. Now you're ready to buy the specific soil amendments required to bring your soil up to snuff.

Tricks of the Trade: The Big Bag of Tricks

I'm a third-generation Major League groundskeeper; my father was field superintendent for the White Sox for 42 years and my grandfather was with the Cleveland Indians for 46 years. I literally grew up on the field at Comiskey Park. I know from experience that your playing field is only as good as your dirt. The turf is important, of course, but since 70 percent of the action in a baseball game takes place on the infield, you better do the dirt thing right.

When I was charged with building the field at new Comiskey Park in 1990, I knew I had to bring the infield skin over from the old park. I had spent too many years conditioning that dirt to perfection for the

(continued)

players to start from scratch at the new park. Plus, my dad had worked magic in that dirt—he practically invented all the great field maintenance tricks that players had been hugging him for (and hating him for) for years.

The late Nellie Fox always said my dad kept him playing for a year or more than he otherwise might have by raising the grass and wetting the dirt by second base. And he kept the baselines raised so Nellie's bunts stayed fair. He was also known to wet down the power alleys when the big-hitting Yankees came to play in Chicago. He'd also soak the area between first and second base when opposing base stealers came to town. The all-time base stealer himself, Rickey Henderson, has belly-ached about my own "soft" basepaths.

My dad taught me to do everything you could think of to make the field work to the advantage of *your* players and against the strengths of the opposing players. In the late 1960s, fans used to call the area in front of home plate at Comiskey "Camp Swampy," because we'd dig it up and soak it with water for our sinkerball pitchers like Hoyt Wilhelm or Tommy John. But if a sinkerballer was pitching for the visiting team, we'd mix the dirt with clay and gasoline and burn it to harden the soil.

I've built sports fields all over the world, including six of the last ten Major League fields. I even built the first natural turf soccer field in Saudi Arabia—that took two Saudi planes full of sod to pull off! The real trick of the groundskeeping trade is to understand the relationship between solid field design, excellent soil and turf development, and smart maintenance. Every ballpark is unique and has its own particular geographic, climatic, and horticultural factors—add to that the habits and requirements of a whole team of players, and you've got a lot of balls in the air. But that's the fun of it.

Roger Bossard
Comiskey Park
Chicago, Illinois

The Squish Test

How do you determine if your soil is sandy, clay, or loam? Just squish it. Take a handful of moist soil and squeeze it in your fist. When you open your hand, check out what the soil does. Sandy soil will break apart easily without any help. Clay soil will actually leak out of your hand as you squeeze it, and you'll be left with a tight lump of smooth soil when you open your hand. Loamy soil will also form a compact lump in your hand, but it easily breaks apart when you poke it with your finger. This is a great opportunity to get the kids involved—let them get good and dirty and learn a little about soil. When you're done just hose them down!

Leveling and Grading the Soil

While you're waiting for the soil sample analysis to come back, use the time to level and grade the soil. Getting this out of the way early will make it easier to mix in any amendments to be sure of an even spread across the topsoil. This will also help get rid of any trenches or depressions in the yard, eliminating the chance of disease or weeds from unevenly drained soil. Also important, a properly leveled lawn will take water and moisture away from the foundation of your house. The time it takes to properly level and grade your lawn can pay off in the long run with fewer of the lawn and foundation problems that excess moisture can cause.

Start by getting your tools together. You'll need a metal garden rake, a shovel, and a wheelbarrow. The garden rake allows you to smooth out and level the soil, and the wheelbarrow and shovel are for moving the soil from one spot to another to even out the grade. You could spend a day or the better part of a weekend on this job, depending on the size of your yard.

These simple steps will help you level and rough grade your yard easily.

1. Before you start, check that the soil is neither too wet nor too dry. Wet soil may be too heavy to work with and dry soil won't want to stay where you put it.

2. Get rid of any debris lying about—rocks, sticks, and any odds and ends that are hanging around. Dig out any larger rocks you find and are able to remove.

3. Rough grade the area. Rake out the yard and see where there are hills or depressions that you'll have to level out or fill in. Even out the hilly areas and use the excess soil to fill in the depressions. If your yard requires considerably more leveling, remove the topsoil and put it aside to add to lower areas or as an additive when preparing the soil for planting.

4. The soil should be higher at the house foundation and gradually slope away from the building to prevent water buildup. The slope should be at an angle of approximately 1 foot for every 50 feet of lawn space. Simply put, the ground should be 1 foot lower 50 feet from the house than it is at the foundation.

These are the first steps in grading your lawn space for planting. The contour of the yard you've created will eventually be the same contour when you're ready to plant. The final grading will be done after all the fertilizer, organic matter, and other soil correctives are added.

Tricks of the Trade: Trees and Turf

"I think that I shall never see a poem lovely as a tree." That's easy for poet Joyce Kilmer to say; he wasn't trying to grow fine turfgrasses on greens, tees, fairways, and home lawns. The tree versus turf controversy rages on golf courses all over the world. Many courses are either already overgrown with trees or are being overplanted with trees for the future, which not only inhibits play but makes the turfgrass struggle to thrive. And if you even *think* about removing trees to improve a course,

(continued)

---

well, you'll hear it from the tree lovers. Obviously, trees are an important landscape and shade factor for home lawns and golf courses alike. But the fact of the matter is you can't have both an abundance of trees with big canopies *and* fine turfgrass. The two just don't go together. Too much shade from the trees and an ongoing battle between the trees and the grass for water make for thin, weak turf. I tell golf course superintendents and home lawn folks the same thing: you have to decide what you want—lots of big trees or a vibrant, vigorous lawn. If you want the trees, get used to the moss or thin grass. And if you want the thick green lawn, you might have to retire a few trees.

James Medeiros

Certified Golf Course Superintendent

Wannamoisett Country Club

Rumford, Rhode Island

Your Level Best

Don't take leveling lightly. The quality of the job you do leveling your yard will affect your lawn and home for years to come. If you can't handle the job yourself, consider hiring a professional. A landscaping company can take care of any extensive digging and soil redistribution that may be too much for the average lawn grower or even a professional like me. When we redid our lawn at home, I knew I didn't have the time, the home equipment, or the knees to do the job the way I wanted to. So we contracted with Barcello & Kane, a great local landscape company. I mapped out the scope of the job for them and provided the seed mix I wanted, and they did a tremendous job on the installation. We looked at it as an investment in doing it properly and saving on some personal aches and pains. For safety's sake—whether you do it yourself or hire out the job—call your local utility companies to be sure any underground wiring or cables are clearly marked to avoid costly accidents. Do *you* want to be the one to blame in your house if the cable goes out?

Preparing the Soil: Compost, Fertilizer, and the Whole Bag of Dirt

Now you come to the point where you make your soil the best it can be. It's time to correct any of those nutrient deficiencies the soil analysis pointed out and to enhance the soil to make it the richest, most inviting soil for your turfgrass seed. Take out your soil test results and let's look at some of the things you might be adding to your soil and why. Follow the recommendations on the soil test results as to the amounts of any of these amendments to add.

Lime and Sulfur

Lime and sulfur help adjust the pH level in your soil. Levels of pH are measured on a scale of 1 to 14, with 1 the most acidic and 14 the most alkaline. For the best lawn, your soil pH should be somewhere in the 6.5 to 7.0 range. According to the soil test, the lab will recommend adding either lime or sulfur to correct the pH. Lime will counter the acidity and sulfur will balance out the alkalinity. Use pelleted lime and granulated sulfur (as opposed to the powdered form of either) as they are the easiest and safest to apply.

Organic Matter

Whether in the form of homemade compost or commercially available compost, organic matter will help sandy soil retain water and nutrients, while loosening and aerating clay soils. Once the lawn is established, this organic matter attracts good microorganisms and worms that will keep your lawn healthy and you happy. Organic matter can be added in the form of compost, sphagnum peat moss, or manure.

Fertilizer Fixes

Soil for a newly seeded lawn requires a different type of fertilizer than an established lawn. Your soil test will indicate the amounts of phosphorus and potassium to add to your soil—don't ignore them. Phosphorus and potassium promote good root development, which is essential to the survival of your new grass. These elements really need to be added to the soil before you plant. You can't go back and add them after the fact and hope they'll improve the roots—they need to be there when the seeds germinate. Nitrogen, which encourages lush foliage, can be added later, when the plants are more mature and the root system can support the fuller leaves.

Gypsum

Gypsum is added to soil in salt-prone areas. It adds calcium, which helps leach the sodium out of the soil for better drainage.

Fertilizer

The soil test should include a suggestion as to what fertilizer to use based on your soil sample. A good starter fertilizer should take care of correcting any phosphorous and potassium imbalances as indicated by the soil analysis. Fertilizer will enrich the soil and create a good base for root growth and nutrient utilization.

Topsoil

There should be a level of 6 to 8 inches of topsoil on your bare yard. If your topsoil level is not that high, you'll need to add some more to ensure a healthy soil bed for good root growth. And remember, not all topsoil is alike. Have a soil test run on your new topsoil, too.

These amendments are available at garden and home improvement centers. If you need a lot of something (such as topsoil or com-

The Math on Dirt

If you need to add topsoil (or any other amendments) to your entire lawn, you need to figure out how many cubic yards of material to buy. For example, to add 6 inches of soil to a 5,000-square-foot lawn, you would need 1/2 a cubic foot of soil for each square foot of yard, or 2,500 cubic feet. There are 27 cubic feet in a cubic yard, so divide 2,500 cubic feet by 27 cubic feet and you end up with the 92.5 (call it 93) cubic yards of topsoil you need for your lawn. And you told your junior high algebra teacher math doesn't matter!

post), purchase it by the cubic yard and have it delivered to your property. The company you purchase it from may also be able to spread it for you (for a price). If not, grab a wheelbarrow and a shovel and get ready for some dirty work.

Thoroughly incorporating these amendments into your soil will ensure a healthy seedbed all around the yard. For best results, you'll need a rototiller, a spreader, and your trusty garden rake to finish preparing the soil.

CHAPTER & VERSE

Mix the amendments well into the soil. The purpose of adding the amendments is to get the best soil possible—so make it *all* the best it can be.

1. If you need more topsoil, add it first. Rototill it into the existing topsoil and subsoil to create a uniform layer.

2. Apply any of the amendments evenly across the soil with the spreader. Set the spreader to apply the concentrations based on the recommendations in the soil analysis.

3. Rototill the amendments into the soil, making sure to get a nice, even layer in all areas of the yard.

4. Using the garden rake, smooth out the soil. Again, check for any small hills or depressions and even them out. The rises won't seem so small when your mower goes over them and the depressions will trap excess water. Once the area has

been raked, use the flat edge of the rake to smooth everything out nice and even.

5. Stand back and admire your work. You've just completed the final grading and you're now ready to plant.

Romancing the Rototiller

If you're an avid lawn guy, the rototiller is one of those pieces of equipment that's very tempting to buy. And the snazzier the machine, the more tempting it is. It's the ultimate garage gadget! But is it really worth it to buy a rototiller to get a good soil base for your new lawn? Unless you're also an avid vegetable gardener, with a lot of space devoted to your garden, probably not. Instead, rent one from a local garden center or rental center and you've got that hotshot heavy-duty piece of equipment that can give your lawn a good starting soil bed. Use it to break up the existing soil during the grading stages and then to mix in any soil amendments before you start to plant. Then return it—let it hog space in someone else's garage!

You know that saying "starting from the ground up"? That's what your soil is, the true foundation of a great new lawn. Spend as much time and resources on your soil as you do on your seed and maintenance, and you'll end up with the lawn you've been dreaming of all along.

SEEDING YOUR LAWN: LET'S PLAY BALL!

3

How to Seed

irst off, you don't need a bunch of gadgets to seed your lawn.

You just need the tried and true tools and supplies that will en-

sure you get even coverage and will keep the seed protected so it

can germinate. Let's look at the tools and supplies you'll need.

Spreader

Of course, you can seed your lawn by hand, but ensuring even cov-

erage with a fist full of seed can be downright tricky. So, now's the

time—if you don't have a spreader, go out and get one. Not only will

you use it to seed your lawn; you're going to need it when the time

comes to fertilize. A spreader has all kinds of nifty settings that allow

Hand Spreader and Drop Spreader

you to determine how much seed should be spread across the soil with each pass. The grass seed package will tell you how to set your spreader to get the best coverage for the kind of seed you've chosen. Some seed is smaller and therefore will require a different setting than larger, denser seed.

So, what kind of spreader do you get? That will be determined by the size of the area to be seeded. Smaller areas can be seeded with a hand seeder. This spreader is usually operated with a rotating hand crank that shoots the seed away from you and onto the soil as you walk along. Walking and cranking doesn't sound too bad, especially for a small area, but be prepared to pay attention so that you get a uniform layer of seed across the lawn.

Medium to large areas (or even small areas if hand-cranking a spreader isn't your style) can be seeded with a drop spreader. This device (also known as a fertilizer spreader) drops the seed through a row or rows of holes at the bottom of the spreader. When calibrated for your grass seed, the holes allow the seed to drop out as you move along. A lever on the handle is connected to a cable that will allow you to shut the holes when you stop or keep them open as you walk along seeding. A drop spreader is a type of spreader for both seeding and fertilizing.

What if you've got a large expanse of yard to cover? A rotary spreader is for you. It works on the same principle as a drop spreader, but the rotary spreader drops seed in a circle instead of a straight line. This allows more seed to be distributed in each pass than with a drop spreader. For extra-large areas, you can rent a large, farm type rotary spreader from your garden center or nursery to make the job that much easier to handle.

Rotary Spreader

Lawn Rake

Once again, your trusty lawn rake makes an appearance. You'll need this for a final soil level check and to mix in your newly dropped seeds.

Weighted Roller

You don't have to buy one of these beauties—you can rent one. Renting is the most popular choice among home lawn growers, as you probably won't need to use it again for a long while—if ever. The weighted roller is a tool with a big drum attached to a handle and is used to tamp down the seed after you've spread it. If you end up becoming a lawn pattern afficionado, you may also use it for patterns. To use, you fill it up with water to add weight, and roll away. You won't have to use much water—if any—to achieve the desired weight.

Water and Watering Device

You'll want to get a watering system together before you plant. Even if isn't going to be your ultimate watering system choice, that's okay. You'll just need to get your hose and a sprinkler or two ready and in the wings. Do not seed until you are sure you have an available water source and a watering strategy so that all of the newly seeded lawn can be reached by the hose or the sprinkler. Set your hoses and sprinklers for a dry run (or is it a wet run?) to make certain you'll be able to water all the corners of your lawn. If you're short or even just a little iffy, go get some more hose.

Mulch

You'll want to protect newly seeded lawn with mulch. This is a very different type of mulch than, say, those red cedar chips you surround your shrubs with. That kind of mulch will kill your new grass seed. You just want to protect it with a light covering of mulch, such as straw or specially designated seed mulch. The purpose of the mulch is to keep your seed from blowing away, protect it from hungry birds and other pesky critters, contain soil erosion, and hold in moisture. A light cover of mulch will do all this *plus* let the grass grow up through it. Seed mulch needs to be biodegradable so it will break down easily and provide nutrients to the new grass once its work as mulch is done.

A few thoughts about different types of mulches. Straw is probably the most popular choice for seed mulch, but don't just hop in the truck and hightail it to the nearest farm for a bale or two. Take care to purchase *weed-free* straw—not hay. Hay from the farmer down the road can contain all kinds of nasty weeds that will choke out your lawn. Buy good straw from a nursery, garden center, or a farm that certifies its straw weed free. One bale of straw will cover about 1,000 square feet of lawn space.

Peat moss is also used as mulch. While it's true that this will protect the grass seed, it is slow to break down and may compete with your new grass for moisture. Commercially developed seed mulches, such as Penn Mulch, work very well in the form of pellets made from paper, and are also available at your lawn and garden center, but may be expensive compared to straw. Finally, burlap may be used, but again, it may be expensive compared to other seed mulches.

Tricks of the Trade: What Americans Want Most

Some time ago, a Harris Poll showed that what Americans wanted most was "green grass and trees all around me." Indeed, green plants provide not only balm for the soul, but are also our best environmental protection, prevent erosion, preserve water, purify the air, and supply oxygen. Carl Sandburg understood this when he said, "I am the grass. Let me work."

I believe that in general we expect too much from natural grass and in return give it too little. We want it to be hardy and beautiful, yet we stress it with overmowing and improper attention to drought and disease. I've been in the turf business for going on 50 years, and I have to admit that many times I don't grow grass by the book—you have to do things your own way. Know your grass and your conditions and do what is best for your turf your way. If it doesn't work, make changes.

A few caveats I never stray from, though, are these:

September and October are Mother Nature's time for growing good grass. If you can only afford to fertilize once a year, September is the time to do it. Seeding at this time is important also. The days are getting shorter, nights are getting longer, and this is what perfect grass growing days are made of.

You can buy the most expensive grass seed available, but if you don't seed or maintain properly, it's all for nothing. You need a soil test,

(continued)

---

rototilling or aerating, and to take the time to make a good seed bed. If you don't, your grass seed will be birdseed.

Mowing is critical to good grass. I have a rule for my grounds crews— if you don't have time to check the gas, the oil, and most important, the sharpness of the blade, you do not have time to mow the grass. One should always mow the grass when the grass wants to be mowed, not when *you* want to mow.

George Toma

Field and Grounds Chief

for every Super Bowl and Pro Bowl ever played

Grass Seed

Don't forget the all-important ingredient—the seed itself! You've decided on the best type of grass based on your climate, the specific conditions of your yard, and the kind of wear and tear you anticipate the lawn having to withstand. You know what kind of seed you want and you know where to get it—but how much seed do you need?

Seed bags are sold based on the number of square feet of area you need to cover. Here's how to figure out the square footage of your yard.

Square or rectangle area—length times width.
Example: 50-foot length x 40-foot width = 2,000 square foot lawn.

Triangular area—base times height, divided by 2.
Example: 50-foot base x 40-foot height = 2,000 square feet; 2000 ÷ 2 = 1,000 square feet.

Circular area—radius (distance halfway across the center of the circle) squared times *pi* (3.14).

Must-Have Seeding Props

Many of the tools you'll need to seed your lawn will be essential later on to maintain your established lawn. Buy quality the first time, as it will save money and aggravation in the long run. These are the tools you absolutely *must* own:

1. Spreader—you'll need your spreader now to evenly distribute the seeds and later to spread fertilizer.

2. Rake—essential now for leveling the soil and then later to rough up the soil in areas when renovating and to rake out soil plugs after aerating.

3. Sprinklers—to help your new lawn germinate and grow and to keep the older lawn alive and in great shape.

4. Mower—you'll give your lawn its first haircut and continue to maintain it with regular mowing.

Here are some additional tools and supplies you'll need:

1. Weighted roller—rent one or purchase one with your neighbors so you all have use of it.

2. Mulch—a one-time purchase for your newly seeded lawn.

3. Seed—buy quality certified seed. Check the label for expiration date, percentage germination rate, cultivars, percentage weed seed, and percentage crop seed. Buy fresh seed and buy only what you need. Grass seed has an expiration date, after which the seed won't germinate properly. Make sure the seed is fresh and *don't* buy more just to keep on hand for next year.

Example: Radius = 30 feet. 30 feet x 30 feet = 900 feet; 900 feet x 3.14 = 2,826 square feet.

Irregularly shaped area—measure the length at the longest point of the area (l). Now measure and mark every 10 feet along this line.

At the 10-foot marks, measure the width of the area at right angles to that mark. Add up all the width measurements and multiply by 10. The resulting square footage is accurate to within 5%.

Example: Width 1 = 20 feet, width 2 = 18 feet, width 3 = 15 feet; 20 + 18 + 15 = 53 x 10 = 530 square feet.

Actually seeding your lawn isn't hard at all. You've got all your tools and supplies, so you're ready to roll.

1. **One more raking.** Give your yard one final rake to remove any remaining rocks or debris and to break up any soil that has compacted over time.

2. **Set the spreader.** Calibrate your spreader per the instructions on your grass seed package and your spreader instructions.

3. **Spread the seed.** Fill your spreader with half the amount you'll need to seed your whole lawn. Start seeding your lawn in straight lines. Once the lawn has been seeded all the way around once, fill your spreader with the other half of the seed. Seed the lawn again, but this time at a 90° angle from your first pass. This will create the uniform spreading pattern you're looking for. Fight the temptation to vary your path and stick to the simple, straight lines.

4. **Resist the urge to overseed.** Sometimes it may not look like you're spreading enough seed. Again, some seeds are smaller than others and may not stand out against the soil. If you overseed, the resulting overabundance of grass plants will be fighting with each other for water and nutrients. This will result in a weak root system, thus inviting disease and disaster to move right in.

5. **Rake in the seed.** Mix the seed into about ¼ inch of the topsoil with your rake. Your seeds will stay put and have a better chance of germinating if they aren't all sitting on top of the soil.

CHAPTER & VERSE

Get all of your tools together before you begin seeding. There's nothing worse than starting a big job and having to stop in the middle because you forgot something. Being prepared isn't just for Boy Scouts.

6. **Roll it over.** Fill the weighted roller about a ½ full, or just leave it empty. Roll over the entire lawn to set the seeds into the soil, ensure proper seed to soil contact, and improve the germination rate. Using any more weight than this can compact the soil too much, restricting the ability of the grass to grow up out of it.

7. **Mulch.** Spread the mulch lightly across the top of the soil. Avoid a heavy hand, as you don't want to choke out the sun from your newly forming grass plants. Cover to only ⅛ to ¼ of an inch. Any more than that and you'll end up raking it off so the new plants can grow up through it. A general rule is not to top dress thicker than the type of grass blade you are working with.

8. **Water, water, and water.** You must water immediately after sowing. A more thorough discussion of watering your new lawn follows later in this chapter.

When to Seed

There are a few conditions to consider when you're getting ready to seed. Where you live (cool season area or warm season area), the type of grass seed you've chosen (cool season vs. warm season or a mixture), the soil temperature, and the weather will all affect your grass seed.

Let's start with where you live and what type of grass you've chosen. If you've followed the discussion on grass seed, you know what climatic region of the country you live in and have chosen seed appropriate for your area. Take into account what you know about these seed types and their growth patterns as grass plants. You don't want to plant grass seed at a time when the plants are naturally slower growing or even dormant. You want to plant seed when the new plants will naturally thrive in certain conditions.

Take cool season grasses. Your first choice for when to plant will be in the late summer to early fall when the grass will take off. The warm days and cooler nights encourage germination, and the plants will have plenty of time to become established before winter and any fall frost will help control annual weeds from getting established. Your second choice for when to plant would be in the early spring. While the conditions are similar, you'll fight more weeds and you may be facing a shorter time for the plants to establish themselves before the onset of the summer heat. If you plant early enough in the spring, your lawn should come in fine.

Warm season grasses are the opposite. They love the heat and dislike the cold. For these types of grasses, sow your seeds in the late spring. They'll have time to germinate and the plants will flourish in the heat of the summer.

The temperature of the soil is a key factor in seed germination and determining the right time to plant. Cool season grasses will have a hard time germinating in the heat of the summer because the soil temperature is too high. Therefore, the cool nights of the late summer and early fall (or early spring) help keep the soil temperature down for seed germination. Warm season grasses, on the other hand, can't stand cool soil. The late spring gives the soil time to warm up so the seeds can germinate properly.

The weather also plays a part when planting your lawn. Choose a time when there's good weather expected for a couple of days. A bit of rain would be helpful, but a hurricane or heavy rainstorm isn't ideal for your seeds. You don't want them washing away into the neighbor's yard after you've done so much work to get them planted. Use your good judgment when picking a day to plant and consider putting off your planting for a day or two if you must to catch the best weather wave.

The Perfect Moment to Seed

The season and the soil temperature have everything to do with the perfect time to seed. There is a perfect season for every grass and a perfect temperature for every seed.

For cool season grasses, you'll plant in the late spring and early fall—just before the height of the growing season. Your second choice is to plant in the early spring, but you may end up battling severe heat and weeds during the summer. The goal is to plant when the soil temperature is from 60° to 75° F.

For warm season grasses, plant in the spring to catch the peak of the growing season. Plant when the soil temperature reaches 75° to 85° F.

Watering and Overwatering

Watering is *the* most important element in the planting process. You can meticulously distribute even amounts of seed across every inch of your lovely soil bed, but without water, those poor little seeds will dry up and never amount to anything. You've done too much work to lose your lawn to dry conditions, so don't plan on taking off on vacation during this crucial time. You don't have to be chained to your hose, but a bit of lawn sitting is required—especially for the first week or two.

Watering immediately after you sow your seeds is vital to start the process of germination. This first watering should be gentle—use a nozzle on your hose (set to a fine mist) or reduce the water pressure to your sprinkler to avoid any harsh spray. You want to just moisten the soil, not saturate it, because the seeds are still close to the top of the soil. There's no reason to drench it because there are no roots you have to reach yet. Moisten the lawn this way three to six times a day until the seed germinates. During very hot or windy weather, water more often as the soil can dry very quickly.

Three words about overwatering—don't do it. Saturating your new seeds can cause the seeds to rot from a disease called pythium blight, which can kill the seeds and destroy your lawn in 24 hours. Overwatering can also cause soil to float, which can create erosion and then there goes your soil *and* your seeds. If you get puddles in the area you're watering, you're overdoing it. Remember—gentle watering is preferable to flooding the soil any day. You may have to water more often, but the results are worth it.

Now, to keep these baby grass plants alive, you still have to water, but not as much. Once you see those little green sprouts all across your lawn, reduce watering to about half the number of times you were watering after seeding. If you were watering four times a day, reduce it to two times a day. You need to water a bit more deeply now that the root system is being developed. Get beyond the surface soil now, and water to a depth of 4 to 6 inches. About the third week after germination, you can drop your watering schedule again and water every other day or every few days if you've gotten rain. The plants are now able to get moisture from deeper in the soil (from the new roots), and deeper soil holds more moisture than surface soil. Thus, there's less watering for you to do. After your new lawn becomes established, develop a schedule of watering—once or twice a week should be fine. Once again, overwatering can stunt root growth at the least, and kill new grass plants at the worst, so keep your eye on the amount of water you're applying.

The Germination Timeline

Different grass seeds have different germination rates. We know, you're waiting and waiting and waiting for your new lawn to come up. Unfortunately, some grasses take longer to germinate than others. On the other hand, you may be pleasantly surprised when you get germination in as little as three days with some species.

Let's take a look at some of the grasses and their time frames for germination.

COOL SEASON GRASSES

Grass Species	Days to Germination
Kentucky Bluegrass	14–28
Rough Bluegrass	6–21
Chewing Fescue	5–14
Red Fescue	5–14
Hard Fescue	5–14
Tall Fescue	7–14
Creeping Bentgrass	6–10
Perennial Ryegrass	3–14
Annual Ryegrass	3–10

WARM SEASON GRASSES

Grass Species	Days to Germination
Bermuda Grass	7–15
Bahiagrass	8–15
Centipede Grass	7–15
Zoysia Grass	10–14

Protecting Your Baby Lawn from Pests, Children, and the Weather

If you've done your job, your baby lawn should be well protected from pesky birds and nasty weather by the mulch you applied after seeding. You may lose some seeds to the birds or a big rainstorm, but your mulch is insurance that the majority of your seeding will stay intact.

The biggest dangers to your new lawn are probably the ones you love the most—the kids and the family dog. Your baby lawn won't tolerate being trod on and dug up on a whim. While it may be impossible to be absolutely sure this won't happen, you can take a couple of precautions to avoid major damage.

First of all, consider getting the kids involved in the process of growing your new lawn. Let them help you seed, mulch, or water. Once they see the fruits of their labor, it becomes more a matter of pride to see the new lawn succeed rather than a need to tromp all over it. Making the new lawn as important to them as it is to you will be more effective than just a stern warning to keep off the lawn.

If the kids are less than enthusiastic about helping you with the lawn, then at least remind them that the new grass is off limits. Rope off the area with brightly colored string or warning tape tied to stakes around the lawn. You can also use metal or plastic garden fencing to delineate the off-limits lawn, but this is a much more expensive option if you've got a lot of area to cover. And it may sound corny, but put up a few signs (Newly Planted Grass—Please Keep Off) so the mailman or unwitting neighbor children don't accidentally quash your dreams of a new lawn.

The family dog is an entirely different matter. All you can do is be sure the dog has a place to walk, play, and "do his business" somewhere other than on your lawn. If there's no other place for him to go, you may just have to bite the bullet and hope for the best. Be sure to pick up any messes he makes as soon as possible. If he does get in there and dig, replace as many of the seedlings as you can. Keep some extra grass seed available for any spots you may need to reseed.

CHAPTER & VERSE

As your grass starts to grow you need to protect it. The plants will recover from a bit of damage, but serious abuse will cause unsightly bare spots that are open invitations to weeds to move in.

Tricks of the Trade: New Lawn

I was recently talking to a contractor, one of those guys who develops big, expensive homes in your formerly quiet, unassuming neighborhood. We were discussing a development of swanky new homes that had popped up not far from my house. I couldn't help asking him why these half-million-dollar homes have 25-cent lawns. It's true. The homes are finished, the lawns are hydroseeded, and what comes up is a little grass and a lot of crabgrass. Here you have an opportunity to grow a brand-new, strong healthy lawn and you blow it with crabgrass. I told him all they needed to do was seed or hydroseed and use an herbicide called Tupersan or siduron. This is not the kind of control that kills both crabgrass and all your new grass seedlings. It's selective for crabgrass and other annual weedy grasses but will not harm the new grass you *want* to see growing in your lawn. In my professional opinion, for the price the homeowner is paying, the developer should go ahead and spend a few extra bucks on a preemergent to control crabgrass in a new lawn.

Kip Tyler

Salem Country Club

Peabody, Massachusetts

Mowing

The final step from a baby lawn to an established lawn is mowing. You can mow your new lawn when it reaches a height of at least 3 inches. By this time, the root system is in place and the soil will have settled enough to withstand the weight of you and the mower. Don't cut off any more than 1/3 of the grass when you mow. Make sure your mower's blades are sharp so that the mower won't be pulling the new grass plants right out of the soil instead of cutting them. A more complete discussion of mowing will follow in chapter 6.

Gentle, careful efforts in the seeding stage make for a new lawn with the best chance to survive and thrive. Take your time, work with the best quality seeds and equipment you can—and be prepared to act like a lawn cop policing the area until your lawn is safely established.

THE MAGICAL
INSTA-LAWN

4

The Science of Sodding

An instant lawn. Sounds like magic, right? Truthfully, there's no magic involved in the making of sod. Sod is just turfgrass

that has been grown on a sod farm. It's essentially the same grass

you can grow yourself, but it's grown under controlled conditions

and someone else is worrying about keeping it watered and safe

from birds and kids. The sod farmer does all the same things you'd

do—water, fertilize, and mow. He just grows the grass in much

larger quantities than you would. When the grass is ready, it is cut

into strips that make the rolls of sod that you buy. No miracle, no

mystery. Just plain old grass.

Why do the sod route then? If you're like most lawn gardeners, there's a burning desire for that thick, green lawn as soon as possible. For instant-gratification types, it could be torture to watch every blade of grass slowly grow from seed. Laying sod gives you that immediate satisfaction. Sod farms usually provide a virtually weed-free product. After all, a weed or two on a sod farm can ruin a whole crop of sod, so the farmers are very weed wary. Sod can also be laid out just about any time of year. The only times it wouldn't be smart to lay sod are during the extreme heat of summer or in the late, late fall when the roots may not have time to establish themselves before the ground freezes. Or, of course, when the ground is already frozen. If you have hilly areas in your yard, you can quickly eliminate erosion with a covering of sod and chances are good it won't wash away like seeds might.

So who wouldn't want an instant lawn? Sod is the lawn gardener's dream—but for a price. Sodding your lawn can cost you upward of 20 to 30 percent more than starting it from seed. However, if you're impatient and are willing to spend the cash, sod is the way to go. Do think twice about using sod if your yard is shady. Commonly, the grass grown for sod is sun loving. Sod farms are wide open—not a stitch of shade in sight—so the grass grown for sod may not survive in your shady areas. In other words, you get what you get and that's that. So if you want sod for your shade, make sure you buy sod grown specifically for shade.

Starting with Sod—Where to Buy, What to Look For

Just because you've decided to sod your lawn doesn't mean you get out of doing your homework before you buy. Just as with turfgrass seed, you need to be sure you're getting a quality product. Sod can be purchased from a nursery, garden center, or directly from the sod farm. Follow these hints when purchasing your sod.

1. **Always buy sod locally.** This way you can be assured that the type of grass grown by your local sod farmer is the same type of grass that will survive in your yard. Local sod will be grown in similar climatic and soil conditions as yours, so your chances for purchasing grass that will survive are best from a local grower.

2. **Get your measurements together.** Don't walk in to purchase sod without an idea of how much you'll need. Measure your lawn space and come up with the square footage. Don't go too crazy about irregularities in your lawn's shape—just measure your lawn in sections and get a good approximation of the total square footage. Add an extra 5 to 10 percent to the total to allow for cutting and shaping the sod to fit any curves or breaks in your lawn space.

3. **Order it.** Be sure to order your sod at least a week before you plan to lay it. This gives the grower time to cut it and deliver it. Don't order it any farther in advance than a week. The sod should not hang around any longer than 48 hours after it's delivered before you lay it. The fresher the sod, the better.

4. **Inspect it.** Unroll a few random sections and check the sod for any weeds, insects, or diseases. If you've gotten the sod from a reputable merchant, you should have a weed-, disease-, and bug-free product. If there is any indication of bugs, disease, or weeds, don't use it. You'll end up fighting a battle you don't want, trust me. Also, any signs of drying, such as browning or curling at the edges, mean the sod is old and already drying out. Don't buy it or take delivery on it. You'll have an impossible time trying to bring it back to life if it's already dying. Finally, check the roots to be sure they're still healthy. They should be white and moist and the sod should be cool to the

touch. Sod that's been cut and sitting around for a while will feel warm to the touch. This is due to decomposition, and the warmth can kill the grass.

When Sodding Beats Seeding

Trying to decide if sodding is the way to go? Besides having the magical insta-lawn in one afternoon, there may be a few reasons why sodding is better than seeding.

1. If you've got a tricky slope in your yard where water runs off, sodding that slope may actually be the most cost-effective way to get grass to grow. Instead of watching your seeds wash down the hill, stake the sod in place and watch it grow.

2. In areas where lawns are hard to establish from seeds, such as shady spots, sod will grow more easily because the grass plants are already mature and can adapt to the shade.

3. Sod won't dry out as quickly as newly developing grass plants. In dry conditions, the soil won't dry out under sod as fast as the bare soil in a seeded lawn will.

4. Sod can be planted at almost any time of the year. If you've missed the time for starting your lawn from seed, you can still get a lawn to grow from sod—as long as the ground is not frozen.

5. Sod can choke out weeds. Any weed seeds that are left in the soil won't stand a chance with a thick carpet of sod on top keeping them from the sun.

6. A properly sodded lawn is ready for average use in about half the time as a seeded lawn.

Laying and Watering Sod

First and foremost, before you lay the sod don't skimp on the soil preparation. Every minute you spend preparing the soil means one less minute of worrying whether your sod will "take." Level, grade, and fertilize your soil just like you would for seeding. If your soil isn't up to snuff, your sod can die just like the seeds would have. Remember, sod isn't a miracle lawn—it's just grass.

When you get your sod delivery, take care of it. If you can't lay it right away, have the delivery person leave the pallets in a shady spot to keep it cool. Water it lightly to keep it from drying out. Sod is best when laid immediately, but it can be kept rolled up for 24 to 48 hours before you lay it down. Leave it hanging around any longer than that and you're just asking for trouble.

Get your tools together. You're going to need a sharp knife for cutting the sod to fit and a wheelbarrow to haul it around. You'll also need to rent a water-filled roller. The sod needs to be rolled to ensure good root contact with the soil. For those slopes in your yard, have a bundle of stakes ready to secure the sod to the ground. Finally, get a board or a piece of plywood so you can stand on *it* instead of your newly laid sod as you work section by section. Finally, get your hose or sprinkler set up so you can water your new lawn immediately after you lay it.

You've got your sod and you've got your tools. Now, here's the fun part:

1. **Decide where to begin.** Choose a straight edge somewhere on your property, such as a driveway or a walkway, from which to start. You will line up the sod against the straight edge and get a good even start to your lawn. If you don't have a straight edge to start with, measure and mark a straight line with stakes and string somewhere in the middle of your yard, so you can lay sod in a straight line on either side of it.

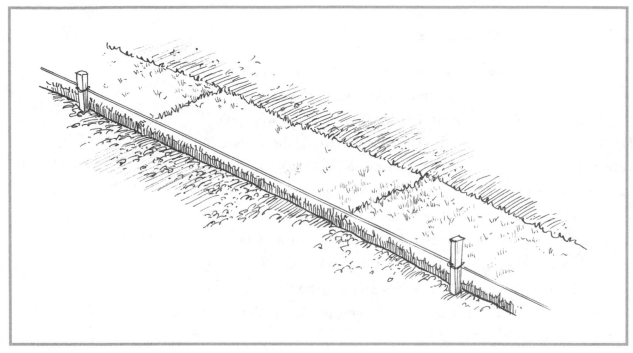

Straight Edge

2. **Work with moist—not soaked—soil.** For best results, the roots of the sod should come in contact with moist and cool soil. Water the soil to dampen it and cool it. Water in sections if you have a large area to cover to ensure you're working with damp soil throughout the project.

3. **Unroll a piece of sod and place it up against your straight edge.** Butt the end of a second piece right up to the end of the first piece—snug, but not overlapping—with no gaps showing and unroll it. Overlapping pieces will cause bumps in your lawn that you'll hate come mowing time, and gaps will leave bare patches as the sod dries that you'll have to fill in. Continue this until you have your first full row of sod. Be careful not to stretch or tear the sod as you lay it. This can cause gaps in the turf as the sod roots to the soil.

   Lay the sod for the second row (and subsequent rows) in a staggered, bricklike pattern to the first row. If you have all the edges of the sod lined up in a row, you'll end up with visi-

Sod in Brick Pattern

ble lines across your lawn. Continue laying all the sod in this fashion, cutting where needed to fit into the space. As you work, avoid standing directly on any newly laid sod. Stand or kneel on your board as you work to evenly distribute your weight across the sod and avoid damaging it.

4. **For those tricky slopes and hills, lay the sod horizontally *across* the slope—never vertically *down* the slope.** Continue the bricklike staggering with each row of sod. For steeper inclines, secure each piece of sod with a stake at both ends so the sod doesn't slide down the hill. Of course, you need to remove the stakes before mowing.

5. **Roll the newly laid sod with the water-filled roller to get rid of any gaps between the sod and the soil.** Fill the roller halfway with water and roll at a 90° angle to the way you laid the sod. Roll the sod in sections if you have a large area to cover so you can water as you go. Tread carefully as you roll to keep the sod in place and the edges even and together.

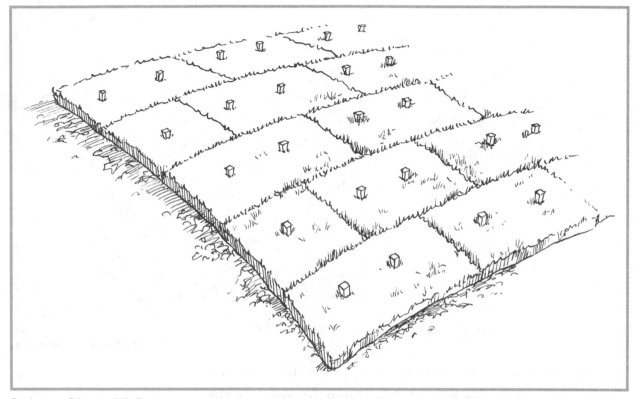

Sod on a Slope with Pegs

6. **Water, water, water.** Newly laid sod should be watered to a depth of at least 3 to 4 inches—meaning the water should penetrate the sod and get into the soil. Watering as you go is a good idea—it'll keep the edges of the sod from drying out too much before you finish the job. Be sure to get all the edges of your new lawn—don't leave any corner wanting for water. When you think you've watered enough, lift a small corner of a piece of sod and check the soil underneath. If you stick a screwdriver in, pull it out, and if it's moist 3 to 4 inches deep—you're done watering for now. If not, keep at it—enough water is essential to protect your investment.

Now that you're new lawn is laid, you still have some work to do. Namely, more watering. You need to water every day for the first week to keep the grass moist. The edges are the first to dry out, so pay particular attention to reaching the edges when you water.

After a week or so, the roots will incorporate themselves into the soil. Now you can start backing off watering every day—say, to every other day—and see how the lawn responds. If all is still green, that's great. If not, keep watering every day for a few more days—especially in hot weather. Keep to watering every other day or so for two more weeks. About three weeks after you laid the sod, drop your watering schedule to a couple of times a week. You should be past the danger of dry spots and be at the maintenance stage of your watering.

CHAPTER & VERSE

Your sod may look like a fully developed lawn, but its survival still depends on you. Proper maintenance after installation will ensure that your insta-lawn will indeed be a lasting lawn.

Tricks of the Trade: The Babe Rests in Peace

Thousands of baseball fans from all over the world make a pilgrimage to Babe Ruth's gravesite every year. And while they're at it, they visit Billy Martin's grave, which is nearby, as well as the graves of actor Jimmy Cagney, gangster Dutch Schultz, and gossip columnist Dorothy Kilgallen, among many other notables.

I don't have the groundskeeping headaches from all of the foot traffic at the cemetery that you might think. For one thing, the Babe's gravesite is in an older, very established section of the cemetery, so there is not a lot of stress to the grass from big machinery that you'd see in newer, more active parts of the cemetery. It's also situated in a fairly open area on a hillside, so visitors make their way to the grave from a variety of directions and don't wear a single path in the grass. Finally, because the grass itself is old and well established, it's not as vulnerable to some of the debilitating conditions that contemporary grass plants might be.

Don't get me wrong, there's plenty of commotion at the Babe's final resting place. Fans leave balls, gloves, bats, baseball cards, game tickets, photos, even personal notes to Ruth himself, creating an ongoing shrine to the Babe. As with all of the graves at Gate of Heaven, we do not disturb the remembrances people leave behind, though we do try

(continued)

to tidy up if the volume gets out of hand. We're also careful to trim around the stones, of course.

It's not just pinstripes we see at Gate of Heaven. We can count on a healthy number of visits from Red Sox fans every year, who come to pay homage in hopes of breaking the curse they believe hangs over the Sox for trading Ruth to the Yankees all those years ago.

Bill Lane

Assistant Superintendent

Gate of Heaven Cemetery

Hawthorne, New York

The Sod Safety Timeline

Avoid excessive traffic on your new lawn. Any step you take on your brand-new lawn can shift the sod, creating gaps. Unless you're prepared to walk, then adjust, walk, then adjust, keep off it as much as possible—especially the first week. Of course you may have to walk on it to water, but don't start having relay races on it just yet. As with newly seeded lawns, rope off the area if you have to.

The way to evaluate your lawn's progress is to check how your roots are doing. After a couple of days, lift up a small corner of a piece of sod. You should feel a bit of resistance as the roots have begun to grow into the soil, but you can still lift it up. Check again in another week. You should feel even more resistance to your tugging. After about three weeks, you won't be able to lift up a corner of the sod anymore. The roots will be fully incorporated into the soil. *Voilá!* This is your new lawn! Of course, the lawn is still tender, so don't have any heavy-duty traffic running across it for a good couple of months.

At this point, your grass should have grown to about three inches or more. Now you can mow. Once again, do not cut off more than a third of the grass. This can inhibit its growth and threaten your new lawn.

Sod Surgery

Before we do sod surgery on an athletic field like Fenway Park we try preventative therapy by overseeding high-traffic areas often with a little seed at a time. However, sometimes because of weather or excess wear we must do sod surgery. Sod surgery is often performed on baseball fields in front of the pitcher's mound, by the on-deck circles, or maybe on the outfielder's spots; on a football field between the hash marks; and a soccer field in front of the goal. At home, sod surgery may be necessary on a heavily used and abused area near a pool or where homeplate is for backyard kickball games. Installing sod is simple if you follow a few tried and true rules. First, make sure you lay the pieces of sod snugly together, staggering the rows. Any gaps in between pieces give weeds the opening they've been looking for to grow. Don't overlap the edges. When the sod pieces grow together, you'll have bumps that'll be a problem when you get to mowing the lawn. If you need to cut the sod to fit in a space, make sure your knife is sharp. You'll want clean edges so the pieces fit together as if they've been cut at the sod farm.

Protecting Your Expensive Outdoor Rug from Pests, Children, and the Weather

The only real pests you'll have to worry about with a sodded lawn are the kids and the dog. The kids? Follow the same suggestions for protecting a newly seeded lawn—keep them off it. While it may look like a mature lawn to them, it's still fragile in the first few weeks.

As for the dog, again, follow the same instructions as for a newly seeded lawn—with one addition. A dog's urine (especially female dogs) can wreck your sod. You'll end up with brown, dead spots before you know it. If you have to let your dog out on your new lawn, you'll just have to watch where it goes. Wherever it urinates, take the hose to that spot. Water it down thoroughly to help flush out the urine from your grass. What you don't want is a concentrated spot of urine penetrating to the roots. It may sound time-consuming, but after all the expense of the sod, isn't a little flushing worth it?

Full Sod Alternatives: Sprigging, Plugging, and Strip Sodding

While sod is by far the easiest way to get a good, full lawn in a matter of weeks, there are other types of lawn planting that can be done besides sodding and seeding. They can be more time-consuming and take longer to become established (up to a year or more), but they are less expensive alternatives to a fully sodded lawn. Many warm season grasses are planted this way, such as varieties of zoysia grass, hybrid Bermuda grass, and St. Augustine grass, as the seeds they produce are sterile and the lawn needs to be started vegetatively. As with any warm season grass seeds, they should be planted in the late spring or early summer.

Sprigging

Sprigging may be the only way to start a lawn with certain varieties of some warm season grasses. A sprig of grass is a piece of a stem of grass or whole stem of grass with no soil attached. It should have three to four nodes from where the roots will develop. A sprig is either planted in a furrow or spread across the soil, pushed in and then tamped or rolled. You can order grass sprigs from a nursery or garden center. They usually come by the bushel, so have your yard measurements ready—the nurseryman can help you determine how much to order.

Planting sprigs can be time-consuming but the more you plant, the less time it will take your lawn to become fully established. Prepare your soil exactly as you would for seed or sod. Don't skip this step. The survival of your sprigs depends on it.

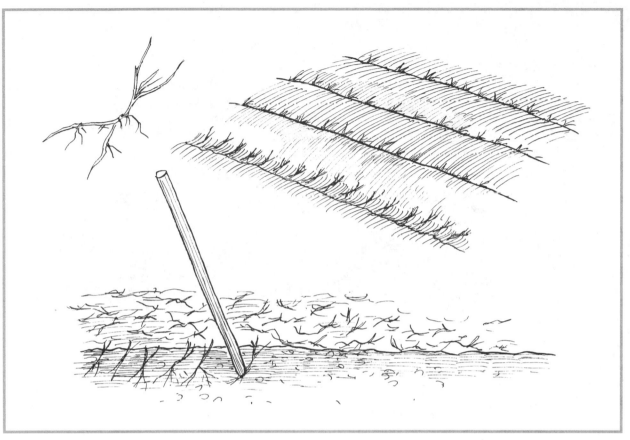

Sprigs in Furrows, Sprigs in Scatter Planting

If planting sprigs in a furrow, dig shallow trenches (furrows) into the soil about 12 to 18 inches apart. Along the furrows, spread the sprigs across the soil, leaving the top leaning upright toward the sunlight. Spread soil across the sprigs, leaving 2 to 3 inches of the sprig exposed, then tamp or roll the sprigs firmly into the soil.

When using the spreading method to plant sprigs, scatter the sprigs across the soil by hand and then poke them into the soil with a stick to a depth of 1 to 2 inches. Spread a thin layer of soil atop the sprigs and then tamp or roll to ensure good contact with the soil.

As sprigs are shallowly planted, you must water them frequently. Water them once or twice a day to keep the soil moist. As they start to grow, you can water less frequently, but any signs of drying should be addressed immediately.

Plugs in Soil Bed

Plugging

Plugging your lawn is sort of like sodding it—but on a much smaller scale. Plugs are actually 2- to 4-inch squares or rounds of sod that are laid out on the lawn, about 6 to 12 inches apart. Once these plugs establish themselves into the soil, they will eventually spread and fill in the bare ground around them. This method can also take up to two years to produce a fully established lawn, but it's a whole lot less expensive than the full sod. Plugs can be purchased from a nursery or garden center, or you can cut your own from sod. Measure out your lawn space so the correct amount of plugs necessary for your lawn can be determined.

Prepare the soil as you would for seed or sod. Dig shallow (2 to 3 inches deep) holes at 6 to 12 inch intervals throughout the yard using a trowel or a bulb planter. If you want a faster-growing lawn, use the 6-inch interval guideline, but the cost will go up as you decrease the amount of space between plugs. Roll the plugs after planting them to ensure the roots have good contact with the soil. As with any other planting method, you must water the new plugs. Follow the same guidelines for watering as for full sod.

Strip Sodding

Strip sodding uses full pieces of sod, but not as many. Therefore, the cost of strip sodding is more than plugging, but not as much as full-out sodding. Lay rows of sod about 6 to 10 inches apart, instead of butting them up right next to each other. They will eventually grow to fill in the bare spots between the rows of sod. Roll the strips as you would sod, and water immediately. Follow the same watering schedule as for full sod.

Now, a word or two about mowing your sprigged, plugged, or strip sodded lawn. Wait until the grass is 3 to 4 inches high before you mow. A sprigged lawn is extremely delicate. If your sprigs begin pulling out of the soil when mowing, stop and wait a week or so more before attempting another mow. If you have to wait, raise your mower blade higher to take off only the top third of the grass. You can mow again in a few days to achieve the desired height for your type of grass.

Mowing plugs or strips is a bit trickier. When the wheels of the mower are on the bare ground and the blade is going over the grass, you're cutting the grass a lot closer than you want to—you're in danger of scalping it. To avoid scalping, raise your mower up higher to compensate for the difference in height between the ground and the grass.

Seeds aren't the only way to start a new lawn. Sodding gives immediate satisfaction for a new lawn, while plugging, sprigging, and strip sodding give you a chance to grow certain types of grass that you couldn't from seed. Whatever method of planting you choose, all of the planning and preparation you've done will make your new lawn a success.

> **CHAPTER & VERSE**
>
> Sprigging, plugging, and strip sodding take longer to establish a full lawn. Be vigilant in maintaining your new grass so that it's at its best to fill in as soon as possible.

THE ABSOLUTE TRUTH ABOUT GROWING A GREAT LAWN

5

G reat lawns aren't made—they're grown. And it's up to you to keep them that way. Watering and fertilizing are the maintenance chores that separate the okay lawns from the truly great lawns.

Your Great Lawn's Best Friend: Mr. Sunshine

Most plants need sunshine to grow—and your lawn is no exception.

Sure, you've got shady spots in your lawn and, if you'll notice, that grass in the shade doesn't do as well as the grass in the sun. Grass needs sun for photosynthesis, where the energy from the sun sets off a complex process by which the plant converts this energy and carbon dioxide from the air into carbohydrates—plant food. Without enough sun, the grass plant can't make sufficient food, which causes stress on the plant and eventually kills it.

So how much sun does your lawn actually need? That depends on the type of grass you've planted. Full sun is at least six hours of direct sunlight on your lawn. Any sun-loving grasses, such as Kentucky bluegrass or Bermuda grass, thrive in full sun. Shade-tolerant grasses, such as a fescue or St. Augustine grass, can survive some shade. Shady areas are the parts of your lawn that receive about three hours or less of direct sunlight. This can be due to sun cover from tree foliage or from the fact that certain parts of your lawn may only receive direct sunlight for shorter periods during the day—shaded by buildings, fences, etc. The good news is that while grass plants mostly love full sun, you can compensate for the lack of sun with proper watering and fertilizing.

Where the Sun Don't Shine

Shady areas need particular attention in your lawn. You have to treat them as separate microclimates or "mini-lawns" within the big lawn. These areas have different requirements for water and fertilizer than areas in full sun, so make sure you're prepared for a little extra work. Once you've planted a shade-tolerant variety of grass in the shady areas, you'll find that they don't need as much water as the rest of the lawn. The shade keeps the soil from drying out quickly, unless there is immediate competition for water from a nearby tree, so keep an eye on the soil in the shade and water accordingly. Shady areas require less fertilizer. The foliage is naturally more lush in shaded areas, so don't overfeed these spots or you'll put the root system at risk for stress.

Tricks of the Trade: Shades of Green

Miller Park has a retractable dome and high walls, so portions of my field get very little sunlight. Early in the year, when the sun is low, certain portions of the field see no sun at all. Growing grass in the shade was something we had to learn how to do.

Grass doesn't like shade. No matter what you do, the grass you grow in the shade will not be as healthy as grass you grow in the sun. But there are at least four things you can do to make your yard *look* better and even *look* good, in spite of the shade:

1. Reduce the traffic on shaded grass. Suggest the kids play ball in other areas of the lawn. Once you have kids playing on it, the grass can't handle the stress.

2. Grow the shade grass a little longer. Most home lawns are mowed to 2 to 2½ inches. If your lawn is 2 inches, I'd raise the shaded portion to 2½. If your lawn is 2½ inches, I'd raise it to 3. This way, the leaf blade will absorb more photosynthetic energy and transfer this energy to its root. The more leaf blade, the better the plant will do in shade.

3. Use a growth regulator. I use Primo, but there are many products on the market. A growth regulator limits the amount of top growth. So, especially in the shade, a regulator keeps the grass from wanting to grow upward and taking its energy upward. The regulator causes the plant to take some of that energy into the roots and rhizomes so it can better handle the light. This produces growth of more plants, rather than growth upward of existing plants. So the grass spreads horizontally and more energy goes into its roots.

(continued)

91

4. Add a biostimulant. We use biostimulants on a regular basis here. It's essentially a complex of amino acids, vitamins, and hormones. The extra amino acids reduce the steps needed in plant growth and recovery. Without the biostimulant, the plant uses its own resources to form the amino acids that the plant needs. If the plant is given the amino acids and doesn't have to use its own energy to produce them, it conserves energy, and stress on the plant is reduced.

Gary Vandenberg

Director of Grounds

Milwaukee Brewers Baseball Club

Milwaukee, Wisconsin

When to Water

There are a couple of different issues involved in determining when to water. The first is when does your lawn *need* water. The second, when is the best *time* to water. Two questions with related answers.

Your lawn will let you know when it needs water. The grass will lose its green luster and turn a blue-gray color. This happens when the blades of grass curl up lengthwise to conserve moisture—the undersides of the blade are lighter in color and that's what you're seeing in that blue-gray cast in your lawn. Your lawn will also lose its ability to bounce back when you walk on it. It will lie flat where you walked, and you'll see visible footprints in the lawn. It may also develop brownish patches—that's an SOS in lawnspeak. You'll see these signs more frequently during hot, dry weather. They can appear very fast, so keep your eyes open for them.

An established lawn really only needs to be watered when it becomes dry, rather than on a regular watering schedule. Different weather conditions, such as temperature, humidity, rainfall, and wind, will all affect the water needs of your lawn. If you water once a week just because somebody once told you that you should, you could be needlessly wasting water and perhaps damaging your lawn in the process. Watering more frequently than your lawn needs can mean more weeds, more disease, and more mowing. Watering only when needed will make maintaining your lawn more hassle free.

Your soil test showed you whether your lawn is primarily sand, silt, or clay and this will determine how often you need to water. A lawn grown on sandy soil may need to be watered three times a week, while one on clay soil may only need to be watered every ten days. Sandy soils don't hold water very well, so the grass will need to be watered more frequently. Clay soil will hold water much better, so less frequent watering is necessary.

What time of the day should you actually water your lawn? Without a doubt, early morning watering is best. You'll diminish the amount of water you waste due to evaporation—both on the grass and directly from the sprinkler. The morning weather is generally cooler, with gentler winds, so the water has a better chance of actually reaching the roots instead of drying up too quickly on the blades or being blown off course by wind. The grass will also have a plenty of time to dry before nightfall, which helps reduce lawn disease.

Watering in the evening or at night increases the chance for diseases to develop in your lawn. A moist environment is the perfect place for some lawn diseases to thrive. If you go to bed with your sprinkler on, you'll wake up to grass that is a virtual laboratory for lawn disease. Watering midday is not the answer either. You lose up to 33 to 40% of those gentle water droplets to evaporation from the sun and wind, which is a waste of water. So just stick with a morning watering routine.

Shady areas need to be watched for dryness, too. You'd think that the lack of sun would keep the soil moist, but your grass may be suffering from drought even without the sun. Grass growing near trees is especially vulnerable to drying out. The roots of a tree will soak up any available moisture, leaving your poor grass with little or no moisture to share. The foliage on trees can also keep rain from falling directly on the grass underneath. Water your shady areas separately from the rest of your lawn if necessary.

Tricks of the Trade: Managing Grass in Shaded Lawns

Shade challenges are the third most common problem for homeowners managing their lawns. (Weeds and poor soil are numbers one and two.) Most grasses don't do well in shade because they are sun-loving plants. Shaded areas have thin turf—which really just boils down to a relatively low number of plants—because none of the plants are really healthy and a little disease or damage can prevent new growth. Reducing the fertilizer amounts by half, applying less water, and mowing the grass at a taller height will often help. Choosing the correct turf species helps, too, if you know the demands that will be placed on it.

I was once asked on a call-in radio show to describe a grass management system for a homeowner with a large oak shade tree in the backyard. After discussing the best fertilizer, water, and mowing methods I recommended planting fine fescues because they have better shade tolerance than most turfgrasses. As she was hanging up, she made a comment about how her dog would like having the turf better than the dirt as the dog spent a large amount of time chained to the tree. I had to jump in and tell her while fine fescue had great shade tolerance, it has poor traffic tolerance. A better choice would be tall fescue: while it may not look as nice as fine fescue, it has both shade and traffic tolerance.

John Stier
Department of Horticulture
University of Wisconsin
Madison, Wisconsin

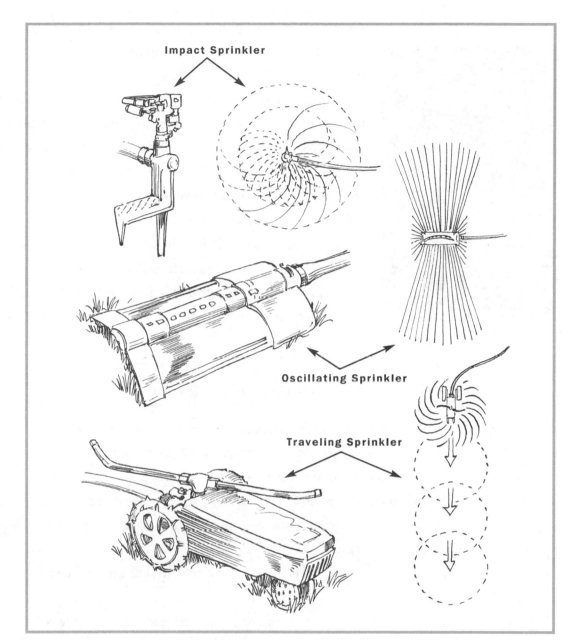

Types of Sprinklers

How to Water

There are two words to remember when determining how to water your lawn—deeply and infrequently. The roots are where all the action is, so you need to water properly to encourage healthy root growth, but not so much as to waste precious water. The same

95

CHAPTER & VERSE

Choose your watering
system wisely. Don't
waste your money on
cheap watering equip-
ment or you'll end up
replacing it far sooner
than you would if you'd
used good equipment.
You get what you pay for.

amount of water applied in smaller amounts more frequently as compared to the same amount applied less frequently can wreak havoc on your lawn.

Consider the root system of your grass. The roots grow as far as they need to to obtain water and nutrients. If you water your lawn only a little bit every three or four days, the roots will be shallow, because the water is only at the top of the soil. While this doesn't sound *so* bad, when the hot, dry summer weather comes, your lawn will be suffering from the lack of water. As the water at the shallow soil level becomes less available, the roots can't go down any farther to search for water. They're stuck, and so are you.

Healthy roots are better able to withstand drought conditions. They can extract moisture from deeper in the soil, even when the

Choosing the Best Watering System for You

I dream of a great automatic irrigation system. Fenway Park is the only ball-park in the Major Leagues with a manual system. Which means that my staff and I have to water the field by hand every time we water. Believe me, I have planned an automatic system for Fenway in my head over and over again. At home, I face different challenges. After moving to New England I immediately encountered the reality of watering restrictions and city regulations on access to water and the cost of drilling a well for an automatic system. There aren't always easy, inexpensive answers.

How do you choose the best watering system for you? First, take a look at your lawn space. By now, you should have an idea of the square footage of your lawn, so don't ignore that information when purchasing a sprinkler system. Get yourself to a good hardware or lawn and garden center and spend some time checking out the sprinklers available. The boxes should indicate how many square feet of lawn the sprinkler will cover, and the method of water distribution.

(continued)

top of the soil dries out. You'll water less frequently and your lawn will be that much more disease resistant. On the other hand, if you err on the extreme side of caution and overwater, you'll be wasting your time and money. The water will go farther down into the soil than the roots need, and you've just wasted good water needlessly. In the worst case, you can be depriving your lawn of much-needed oxygen by keeping the soil drenched, and the roots can actually drown and your grass will die.

How Much to Water

Water your lawn until the water reaches between 6 to 8 inches deep into the soil. You can check this by poking a long screwdriver into the soil after watering. If it goes in easily to a depth of 6 to

Impact sprinklers throw a pulse of water in a circular pattern. Some impact sprinklers allow you to adjust to only a portion of the circle to water in smaller areas. Oscillating sprinklers throw water from an arm that moves back and forth in an arch across the area, usually in a rectangular pattern. They throw water higher in the air, so water can be lost to evaporation as the sprinkler arm moves through the highest point of its motion. Traveling sprinklers move slowly along a length of hose positioned on the lawn. A revolving sprinkler head is attached to a small tractor that runs along the hose you've set up. This sprinkler throws water in a circular pattern also, but the movement of the tractor along the hose allows you to cover a longer area without having to move the sprinkling device.

Finally, in-ground sprinkler systems are permanent irrigation systems that will water the entire lawn area with a flick of a switch. Expensive, yes. But permanent, too, and an excellent way to consistently and efficiently water your lawn. Toro and Hunter are both quality brands. If you're thinking of an in-ground sprinkler system, check your town regulations to determine if you can use town water or if you will need to drill a well.

8 inches, you're all set. If not, keep at it until the moisture in the soil reaches down to that optimum level.

Check the absorption rate of your soil to determine the amount of time you need to let the sprinkler run so that you know the water is getting down into the soil and not just running off the top. For instance, clay soils are slow to absorb water. If the water is puddling or running off, it means the soil can't soak up the water at the rate the sprinkler is delivering it. You'll need to water clay soils in cycles. Water the lawn until you see some runoff, then shut off the sprinkler or move it to another location. Let the water absorb into the soil, then move the sprinkler back to the original spot and water again until the full amount has been applied.

For sandy soil, the water won't run off, but will be absorbed so quickly that it can bypass the roots if too much water is applied at one time. Again, water in cycles to prevent wasted water. Water sandy soils in 1-inch increments. Check how much water is being

---

Tricks of the Trade: A Fish Story

I have had the distinct honor to follow in the footsteps of the legendary Red Sox groundskeeper Joe Mooney. Joe tells some incredible stories from his 30-plus years with the Red Sox and before that in Washington, D.C., where he worked at RFK stadium with Vince Lombardi. When I first started at Fenway in January 2001, Joe and I discussed how different every major league park is, each with its own unique challenges with weather, microclimates, events, and drainage idiosyncrasies. He began talking about drainage at Fenway and said that sometimes, if it rained really hard, fish from the Charles River would come out of the first base camera pit and swim out onto the field. Like I said, Joe's a storyteller, and I thought he was pulling my leg to see how the new guy would respond.

(continued)

---

delivered by your sprinkler to determine the time it takes to water 1 inch. Place a can or pot under your sprinkler spray. Note the time it takes to fill the container with 1 inch of water. That's the amount of time it will take your sprinkler to apply 1 inch of water.

Now, figure out how much water your sprinkler is putting out so you know how long to water each section to reach the full amount of water needed. Using the same method to determine how long your sprinkler takes to apply 1 inch of water, you can determine how much time it needs to be in place in any one area. If your sprinkler delivers ½ inch of water every 30 minutes, you know you have to water an area for one hour to reach the 1-inch mark.

Finally, unless you've got an underground sprinkler system that can water the entire lawn at one time, make sure your sprinkler patterns overlap. Sprinklers may not have even distribution around the whole targeted area, so place a few cans around it to test it. Put one about a foot away from the center of the sprinkler, another three

A few months later, on the Friday night and Saturday morning before Opening Day, Boston got 2½ inches of rain. When the rain finally stopped around midmorning, I went onto the field to inspect the condition of the grass. I started in the outfield and made my way to the infield tarp edge. About 10 feet deep in the outfield, I spotted something that was, to my huge amazement, an 8-inch bass. I immediately looked up into the stands to see if Joe was looking. I was sure I was on *Candid Camera,* that it was a total setup. Joe was nowhere to be seen, though, and the more I looked around, the more bass I found. There were a total of eight fish on the field at Fenway that day.

Looking back I wish I had done two things. First, I wish I had taken photos of this extraordinary scene, so that when I tell this story to the groundsmen who follow me, they'll know I'm not telling a whopper. And I also wish I had mounted one of those bass to hang in Joe's office.

David Mellor

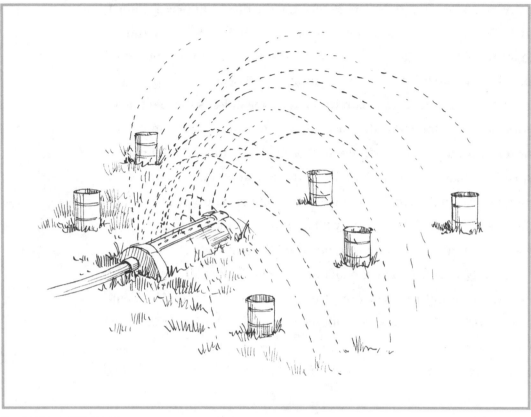

Sprinkler with Cans

feet away, and the third at the edge of the watering area. You can then decide where you have to overlap the watering areas as you move the sprinklers around the lawn to get full and even coverage. When moving the sprinkler from one area to another, position it so that the outer edges of the watering area overlap the previous watering area just a bit. That way you won't get that dry, brown strip of lawn in the center of your yard because of careless sprinkler placement.

With all the concerns about root growth and watering frequency, figuring the amount of water your lawn needs is easy. Turfgrass needs about 1 to 2 inches of water a week. That's total—including rainfall. Use a rain gauge to determine how much rain has fallen so you can supplement that water with your sprinklers. If there is no rainfall, you'll have to water the full amount with the sprinkler.

The amount of water your lawn needs can change during the seasons. In the heat of the summer, some turfgrasses may turn yellow and go dormant. That's normal. The plants are perfectly capable of taking care of themselves when dormant. During these times, however unattractive it is, you can leave them dormant until the rain comes. They'll spring back to life in no time. If you insist on watering to keep the lawn that bright green, you'll have to use more water to keep it that way. Just remember—water deeply and as infrequently as your lawn can handle.

Tricks of the Trade: Sprinklers On, Sprinklers Off

Lawns in Colorado and the western United States require frequent irrigation if they are to remain green and growing during the summer months—as often as three times a week. Because of differences in grass species, soil type, irrigation systems, water delivery rates, etc., it is difficult to say how long you should leave a sprinkler on. I usually suggest my "Easy Lawn Watering Technique." First, look for signs of drought stress in the lawn, which will appear as patches of gray/blue-green grass with a wilted look. "Footprinting" is also a sign of drought, where the grass doesn't bounce back within a short time after you walk on it, leaving footprints with a wilted look all over the lawn. Once you recognize these signs of the need to irrigate, apply $1/2$ to $1 1/2$ inches of water uniformly over the lawn—stopping when water begins to puddle or run off into the street. Then water again when you see new signs of wilt. The frequency of irrigation will vary from week to week, depending upon temperature, relative humidity, cloudiness, and wind. Instead of putting your irrigation clocks on autopilot, turn them on and off manually. This results in a healthy lawn and can substantially reduce water use.

Dr. Tony Koski

Extension Turf Specialist

Colorado State University

Fort Collins, Colorado

Dormant or Dead?

Grass can go dormant or even die from a lack of water. With the increasing instances of water restrictions around the country, one of the first "luxuries" to go is lawn watering. During drought conditions, your lawn will suffer, but how do you know if your grass has gone dormant or actually expired? The truth is, you'll have to wait and see. Once the drought is over and you've gotten some good soaking rains, you'll either see your grass start to come back to life or it'll stay that awful brown bristly stuff. It's going to take more than one soaking for your grass to recover from dormancy, so wait for a few good rains before you panic because your grass hasn't come back. If indeed, the grass doesn't recover, you can seed those spots with a more drought-resistant variety of grass.

Lawn Food: The Chemical Features of Fertilizer

There are 16 different elements your lawn (or any other plant for that matter) needs to grow. Some are plentiful—carbon, hydrogen, and oxygen—from the air and water. Others are found in the soil and some will need to be fed to your lawn with fertilizer. That's right—you need to *feed* your lawn. Those millions of grass plants growing in your yard are all hungrily vying for the same food supply. When there's not enough to go around, some will suffer and die off, others will just manage to limp along, and the hardiest will survive. Meanwhile, weeds will move right in when space from dead or weak plants becomes available. If you want all of those plants to survive and keep weeds out, you must feed your grass.

In order to thrive your lawn needs carbon, oxygen, hydrogen, nitrogen, phosphorus, potassium, calcium, magnesium, sulfur, iron, manganese, copper, boron, zinc, chlorine, and molybdenum. I know you can hardly keep up with the vitamins and minerals your own body needs, never mind your lawn's long grocery list! It is daunting to think that your lawn must have all of these elements in sufficient supply to grow. Luckily, many of the elements are needed in trace amounts, so you don't have to be concerned with providing every last one of them. These elements (excluding the abundant oxygen, hydrogen, and carbon) are broken up into three categories in order of importance—macronutrients, secondary nutrients, and micronutrients.

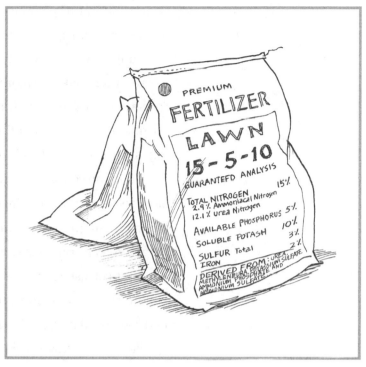

Fertilizer Bag

The macronutrients are the top elements necessary when fertilizing because your lawn uses them in the greatest quantities: nitrogen, phosphorus, and potassium. Those big numbers on all the fertilizer bags, like 15–5–10, represent the ratio of nitrogen, phosphorus, and potassium by weight in the product. No wonder the numbers are printed so big on the bags—it's major information for you and your lawn.

Nitrogen (N)

Nitrogen is the most important element that your lawn needs. It aids in rapid shoot growth and keeps your lawn a healthy, rich green. So nitrogen is the element that is added to your lawn in the largest quantities. If your lawn is nitrogen deficient, it will turn yellow and wither. Nitrogen also leaches out of the soil at a rapid rate, so a steady supply of nitrogen is hard to keep in the soil when applied in small quantities.

While all of this might sound terrific and you're ready to run out and buy a bag of nitrogen, beware that there really can be too much of a good thing. Overfeeding your lawn nitrogen can injure your plants and "burn" your lawn. Additionally, excess nitrogen can cause a major growth spurt in your lawn. This means *much* more mowing (like any of us have time for that) and creating a habitat for a bunch of creatures that love to munch on a long, lush grass plant. Since nitrogen leaches through the soil easily, water runoff containing this surplus nitrogen can end up polluting the groundwater or nearby lakes and streams. That's too high a cost for overzealous fertilizing.

The source of nitrogen in fertilizer will either be fast release, slow release, or a combination of the two. Your lawn will still get nitrogen no matter what source you choose, but the effects of the nitrogen release on your lawn will differ with each type.

Fast-release fertilizers will have ingredients such as ammonium sulfate, ammonium phosphate, and urea. The nitrogen in these products gets used up quickly, as it is available to the plant as soon as you spread it. Your lawn will react immediately to this type, but the effects are short lived. Your lawn will green up with the initial intake of nitrogen, but once it passes through the soil, it's gone. It is water-soluble so it passes through quickly. With the immediate availability and concentration of nitrogen in these fertilizers, this is the most likely type to burn your lawn because of their high salt content. The chance for water contamination is also higher with this type of product. This is the least expensive type of fertilizer you can buy, but you may have to apply it more often to replace the lost nitrogen.

Slow-release nitrogen in fertilizer will be in the synthetic forms of urea (IBDU *isobutylidin diurea*), sulfur-coated urea (SCU), poly-coated, or organic materials such as animal manures or sewer sludge. Both the synthetic and the organic forms of nitrogen are released slowly to the plant, but for different reasons. The synthetic form has a coating around the nitrogen that will dissolve slowly. Manufacturers have developed these coatings so that they will dissolve at different rates, thus releasing the nitrogen into the soil over a period of time instead of all at once. Organic forms require microbes in the soil to process the nitrogen (which happens over time.) Both of these types of fertilizers are more expensive, but will require fewer applications and have longer lasting results.

Many fertilizers available today are a combination of both fast-release and slow-release nitrogen. These provide the best of both worlds—grass will green up more quickly and will stay greener longer. The chance for nitrogen damage to your lawn or for water contamination is lessened. The price should also be just about right.

Tricks of the Trade: Watering in Water-Restricted Times

Being in charge of the only Major League field that doesn't have an automatic irrigation system puts a lot of pressure on me *and* the grass. People always ask me how I manage without it and I always answer that it's not easy. The club, the players, the fans (a.k.a., Red Sox Nation), and I want the best playing surface possible, but the New England weather combined with the radiant heat off Fenway's famous Big Green Monster really stresses the grass and stretches our resources in watering the grass. A recent addition to my water management practice at Fenway and in my new home lawn is a terrific wetting agent (surfactant) product called Aqua-Maxx. I can honestly say this product has been a huge asset to me at the Park and a great help during the grow-In period when I installed our new lawn last fall.

This product is newly available to the home lawn care customer, and I predict that wetting agents like Aqua-Maxx will become an integral part of the future of home watering practices. Aqua-Maxx combines the qualities of the wetting agents used in soap and shampoo with the plant protein power of kelp, which together are a powerful treatment for your lawn. This surfactant helps you grow stronger, more drought- and disease-resistant grass using less water. It maximizes the water that you apply to your lawn by making sure it gets into the soil and doesn't sit around at the surface only to evaporate. Because your soil gets and retains more water at each soaking, the lawn requires less frequent

(continued)

watering. When used regularly, your lawn will develop a stronger root system and perform better under tough conditions.

Most people who care about their lawns care about the enviroment as well. As we look into a future where lawn watering restrictions will certainly become the norm, wetting agents and other smart water gathering, retaining, and dispersing techniques will be key to a healthy, green lawn.

David Mellor

Phosphorus (P)

Phosphorus is essential for root and shoot growth. It is usually present in sufficient quantities in the soil—especially if you added it to the soil before planting. In fertilizers, it is in the form of phosphate (P_{2O5}) and will not absorb into the soil with water like nitrogen. It takes a while for phosphorus to reach the roots, so your best defense against a phosphorus deficiency is to incorporate it into the soil before you plant. Having said that, the phosphorus in fertilizer won't hurt your lawn when applied properly using the result of the soil test as your guideline.

Potassium (K)

Potassium is necessary to keep your lawn resistant to weeds, disease, healthy overall. It is the all-in-all lawn health booster. It helps your lawn better withstand heat and cold, drought, and wear. Potassium, supplied by potash (K_{2O}) in fertilizers, can be applied in smaller quantities. Fertilizers with more potassium are recommended for sandy soils. It's hard to know when your lawn has a potassium deficiency without testing your soil, but applying it regularly is a good bit of lawn insurance.

Secondary Nutrients

The secondary nutrients—calcium, magnesium, and sulfur—can usually be found in sufficient quantities in the soil. If your lawn's pH is out of whack, lime is applied to supply calcium and magnesium to raise pH, while sulfur is applied to lower it. Your soil test will help you determine if you need to add these elements.

Micronutrients

Iron, zinc, manganese, copper, molybdenum, boron, and chlorine are also usually available from the soil. Without a soil test, you may never know if your lawn is deficient in any of these elements—with the exception of iron. An iron deficiency will turn your grass yellow and is most likely to occur in soils with a high pH. Many quality fertilizers will contain iron.

What to Feed

The most important thing you can do before fertilizing your lawn is get a soil test. As discussed in chapter 2, you can't know what is or isn't in your soil until you have it tested. Even if you've had an established lawn for a while, it's good to get your soil tested every two to three years because your lawn's needs may change. Once you've determined deficiencies in your lawn, you can adjust with fertilizer. Choose fertilizers with the recommended amounts of whatever elements you need. If you have to change your soil pH, add lime or sulfur in the proper amounts. The recommendations section of the soil test will tell you exactly how much of what nutrients you should apply.

If you're just going to wing it, you can go ahead and fertilize without a test. If you do this, at least understand some grass basics when it comes to choosing what to use for fertilizer. Since the most important element you'll need to add is nitrogen, you want to figure out the nitrogen needs for your particular type of grass. These are some guidelines for nitrogen needs of different grass species. If you want a lower maintenance lawn, use the smaller amount. If you're willing to work with a higher growing grass, opt for the larger amount.

Grass	Pounds of Actual Nitrogen Needed per Year per 1,000 Square Feet
Bahia grass	2–4
Bentgrasses	3–6
Bermuda grass	2–6
Blue gramagrass	1–2
Buffalo grass	1–2
Centipede grass	1–3
Fine fescue	1–3
Kentucky bluegrass	3–6
Ryegrass	2–3
St. Augustine grass	3–6
Tall fescue	2–4
Zoysia grass	2–4

Fertilizer—Where to Buy, What to Look For

Buy your fertilizer at any reputable garden store, nursery, or lawn care center. The prices may vary from place to place, but be sure you're comparing like ingredients when comparison shopping. Going for the best buy is not smart if you're not at least prepared to look at the label. There is certain information that is required by law to be on all fertilizer labels. Making sense of all of this information will be easier when you know what it all means.

The first thing you'll see is the guaranteed nutrient analysis. Those three numbers represent the ratio of nitrogen, phosphorus, and potassium by weight in the package. For example, a ratio of 15–5–10 is a ratio of 3 parts nitrogen to 1 part phosphorus to 2 parts potassium. Although not required by law, most quality fertilizer will have the breakdown of nitrogen types listed also. You can see exactly how much of what types of nitrogen (fast-release or slow-release) are in the package.

Now, you can figure out exactly how much nitrogen and other nutrients are actually in the package. Take the weight of the package and multiply it by the percentage of the nutrients in the analysis. A 100-pound package of 15–5–10 fertilizer will have 15 pounds of nitrogen, 5 pounds of phosphorus, and 10 pounds of potassium. You now know the total amount of nitrogen contained in the fertilizer so you can buy it according to how much nitrogen you'll need to apply to your type of turfgrass. You will probably be fertilizing your lawn more than once a year, so be sure to divide the number of pounds of nitrogen you'll need for the whole year by the number of times you'll fertilize to get an accurate number of pounds you'll have to buy for each application. For example, if you want to apply 2 pounds of nitrogen per application to each 1,000 square foot of lawn and you have 2,500 square feet of lawn to cover, you'll need 5 pounds of nitrogen per application. If you fertilize four times a year, you'll need a total of 20 pounds of nitrogen for the entire season.

Other ingredients, such as the secondary and micronutrients, are also listed on the package label. The percentages of each of these additional nutrients are shown so you know exactly how much of each you'll be applying with that product. So, what's in the rest of the package? Well, it's a kind of filler—a *carrier* actually. These are inactive ingredients that the nutrients cling to to help carry them through the soil.

What if your soil test has determined that you don't need all three of the major nutrients in your lawn. While a *complete* fertilizer contains all three, you can purchase fertilizer without any phosphorus or potassium if your lawn doesn't need it. You'll have to add nitrogen anyway, so you can purchase a 21–0–0 or a 33–0–0 fertilizer for just the nitrogen.

The type of fertilizer you choose—dry or liquid—is really just a matter of personal preference. The fertilizers discussed in this chapter are the dry types, just because they're the most popular type of fertilizer. Liquid fertilizers are more difficult to apply evenly because they're hand-held and you must stop repeatedly to refill the attached hose-end sprayer. If you want to use a liquid fertilizer, be sure to follow the manufacturer's instructions for proper application.

To determine how much fertilizer you'll need to buy, you'll need the square footage of your yard that you figured out for planting. Almost all fertilizer applications are calculated per 1,000 square feet. If your lawn is 3,000 square feet and the package you're looking at has one 1,000-square-foot application, you'll need three packages or one larger one. Don't have a "more is better" attitude when it comes to fertilizer. Feeding more nutrients than your lawn needs can harm it—like an overdose of nitrogen. The safest amount of fertilizer to buy is what is based on your soil test report and by the amount of nitrogen your particular grass type needs for optimal growth—and no more.

When to Feed

When to feed your lawn is actually a question in two parts— what time of day is best to feed and what times of year you should feed. Let's start with the easy one. The best time of day to fertilize is when the grass is dry. Fertilize the lawn, then water it to knock the fertilizer off the blades of grass and activate it into the soil. Don't fertilize on wet grass—as the grass dries, the fertilizer left on the blades can actually burn the grass in the hot sun.

Next comes the tricky part—what times of year you should fertilize. You've probably heard all the theories—fertilize in spring,

The Clippings Controversy

One of the liveliest lawn-related arguments going is whether you should leave your clippings or rake them up. I love clippings; I leave them on the field at Fenway and on my home lawn. If you leave your grass clippings on the lawn after you mow, the nitrogen in those clippings gets released back into the newly cut lawn. Just by leaving your clippings, you can reduce the amount of nitrogen you have to add to your lawn by up to 25 percent. Of course, the amount of nitrogen your clippings provide depends on how much you fertilize. For instance, even if you only fertilize on the low end of the scale for your grass type, the nitrogen contained in those clippings can add up to $\frac{1}{2}$ pound of nitrogen a year per 1,000 square feet. If you're on the higher end of nitrogen application, your clippings could add a whopping 2 pounds of nitrogen per 1,000 square feet back into your lawn. Just think of all the money you can save on fertilizer! And don't worry about thatch—grass clippings don't turn into thatch. They break down pretty quickly—you can see the results of the nitrogen release from clippings about a week after you mow.

fertilize in the fall, fertilize in both seasons. Well, these theories are right, *and* they are wrong. Fertilization times truly depend on what type of grass you're growing. How's that for a non-answer? Thankfully, you *can* follow one general rule of thumb when determining when to fertilize. Fertilizing will be most beneficial before the period of active growth of your grass. For cool season grasses, this is usually in the spring and fall. Warm season grasses will benefit from a feeding in the late spring through the summer.

A spring feeding for cool season grasses, such as Kentucky bluegrass and fine fescues, will help the lawn green up for the season and gives the lawn time to grow before the summer slowdown. Having said that, fertilizing too early in the spring will encourage major foliage growth when the root growth can't keep up. Fertilizing too late in the spring (especially with a fast-release fertilizer) will encourage rapid growth right before the heat of the summer. During the hot summer, the grass may not be able to withstand the frequent mowing required, never mind the water required to maintain this new growth. A fall feeding for cool season grasses is recommended to promote the growth the grass will need to sustain itself during the winter. It will encourage a longer growing season, which will help the grass store up carbohydrates for a quick greenup in the spring.

Warm season grasses grow most during the summer, so generally you'll want to fertilize in the late spring and the summer. Be careful not to fertilize too late into the summer or into the fall. Feeding during these times promotes lush growth that may make your lawn more vulnerable to winter injury when the cooler temperatures of winter arrive.

How to Feed

Fertilizing is best done with a spreader. It's very difficult to use a handheld crank spreader to accurately fertilize, so don't even think about it unless you have only a very small area to cover. As noted earlier, invest in a good spreader. A rotary or broadcast spreader will give you an even application and help you avoid unsightly greenup.

The package of fertilizer or your spreader instructions lists application settings for spreaders. The problem is that the fertilizer bag may not have a listing for your type of spreader or you've lost the spreader instructions. So, if you can't get the information necessary to set your spreader to the correct application rate, you'll have to calibrate it. It's not a fun thing to do, but it can save you a few bucks if you don't want to buy a new spreader. With all the things that can go wrong when you overfeed your lawn, you don't want to accidentally do it because your spreader wasn't adjusted properly.

To calibrate a drop spreader:

1. Measure the width on your spreader—the bottom part where the fertilizer is distributed. Common spreader widths are 1, 1½, and 2 feet.

2. Attach a catch pan or a V-shaped piece of cardboard to the bottom of the spreader with some wire to catch the fertilizer as it comes out of the spreader during you test.

3. Measure and mark off a distance for your test—20 feet, 50 feet, or 100 feet. The longer the distance, the more accurate the reading. Don't do this test on your lawn—use a driveway or a flat, paved area to protect your lawn from accidental spillage.

4. Close the hopper and fill the spreader with fertilizer.

5. Start about 10 feet away from your measured test distance and begin walking at your normal pace. At the beginning measure mark, open the hopper, then continue walking at the same pace to the end of your measured test distance. Close the hopper when you reach the end mark.

6. Collect the fertilizer from the catch pan and weigh it.

7. Multiply the width of your spreader by the distance of your test area. This is the total square feet of area covered.

8. The rate of application for your spreader is the number of pounds of fertilizer in the catch pan for the area covered. For example, a spreader that is 2 feet wide, tested on a 100-foot measured area covers 200 square feet of area. If you weighed out 1 pound of fertilizer from your catch pan, you're applying 1 pound of fertilizer to 200 square feet of lawn. Fertilization application rates on packages are figured by 1,000 square feet, so your spreader will use 5 pounds of fertilizer to cover 1,000

square feet—1,000 square feet ÷ 200 square feet = 5 x 1 pound of fertilizer used = 5 pounds.

9. Repeat these steps as necessary to correctly calibrate your spreader to the application rate recommended for the fertilizer you are using.

10. Clean up test area.

11. If you don't want to go through this hassle, it might be time for a new spreader. Remember—keep the instructions for this one.

To calibrate a rotary or broadcast spreader:

1. Put some fertilizer into the spreader and be sure the hopper is closed. Open the hopper, walk along a driveway or other paved area (not the lawn) and measure the width of the area covered by the spreader. This is your distribution width.

2. Empty the hopper.

3. Choose a test distance that when multiplied by the distribution width equals 1,000. For example, if you have a distribution width of 10 feet, measure out and mark a distance of 100 feet for a total of 1,000 square feet of application area.

4. Fill the hopper with 5 pounds of fertilizer.

5. Starting 10 feet away from your beginning mark, walk at a normal pace and open the hopper when you reach the starting mark. Shut the hopper when you reach the end mark.

6. Empty the fertilizer that remains in the hopper into a garbage bag. The bag won't add any additional weight to the remaining fertilizer like some buckets will.

7. Weigh the bag. Subtract the amount the bag weighs from your original 5 pounds of fertilizer and this is the amount of fertilizer your spreader will apply for every 1,000 square feet.

8. Repeat these steps as necessary to calibrate your spreader to the recommended application rate for your fertilizer

9. Clean up test area.

If you were lucky enough not to have to calibrate your spreader, there's still one test you have to do. To be sure your spreader will distribute the fertilizer evenly through all the holes in the hopper, check the distribution pattern. Put a small bit of fertilizer in the hopper and walk the spreader down about 5 feet of driveway. The distribution of the fertilizer should be nice and even across all of the covered area. If you notice stripes running lengthwise throughout a portion of the coverage area, you've got a couple of clogged ports. If you have horizontal skips across the coverage area, you've got some material clogging the ports that occasionally gets dislodged, then clogs up again. In either case, clean your spreader thoroughly to ensure proper application rates.

Now, you have the spreader all calibrated for your fertilizer and you're ready to zoom out across the lawn like a fertilizing fiend. Hold on though—you still need a plan of attack.

1. Fill your spreader somewhere other than on the lawn so you won't accidentally spill a load onto your precious grass.

2. Make two passes (header strips) at both ends of your lawn so you can turn around easily at the end of each pass. For irregularly shaped lawns, make one header strip all around the edge of the lawn. Also make header strips around any flower beds, trees, or buildings in the middle of the lawn.

3. Fertilize in straight lines down the long area of your lawn—there's less turning to do that way.

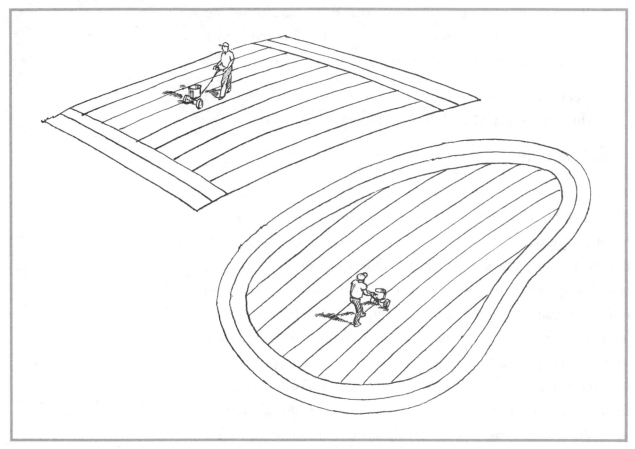

Fertilizer Application Patterns

4. Close the hopper when you reach each header strip and open it again after you've turned around to begin the next pass.

5. Align your wheel marks to overlap each other for drop spreaders. For rotary spreaders, overlap the application area by a couple of inches from one pass to the next.

6. Be sure to keep a constant pace as you walk. Walking too slowly can apply too much fertilizer during each pass, and walking too fast can minimize the amount of fertilizer you put down.

7. Lightly water the lawn to bring the fertilizer from the top of the grass into the soil.

8. If you do spill fertilizer on the lawn, pick up as much as you can immediately. Flush the area *very* well with water.

9. Sweep up and dispose of any excess fertilizer that ended up on driveways, walkways, or the street to minimize the risk of pollution.

Tricks of the Trade: Lime Green

Some years back I had a little experience maintaining the infield of a Pony League park. My radio partner, Jim Zoppo, recommended that I lime the field early. So I limed above the snow cover in February of that year. When the grass came out in spring, it was green as can be. And it stayed green throughout the summer, even during an unusually dry June and July. It takes four or five months to really see the benefits of lime. Do it early and watch it green.

Moe Lauzier

Talkhost and baseball fanatic

The WRKO Gardening Show

Brighton, Massachusetts

CHAPTER & VERSE

Be sure to spread your fertilizer evenly across the lawn. Areas that don't get enough fertilizer will be obviously less lush when the rest of the grass begins to grow and green up. Not only is it unsightly, the underfertilized grass won't be as healthy as the surrounding lawn.

How Often to Feed

How often should you fertilize? This is where your preference in maintenance levels comes in. Decide how often you want to mow, how much watering you want to do to maintain that lush green color, and how many times you actually want to *have* to fertilize. You know you'll probably have to fertilize your lawn at least once a season to keep it alive, but it's up to you as to how much growth you really want for your lawn.

If you want a low-maintenance lawn, fertilize only once or twice a year. For cool season grasses, fertilize once in the fall. Warm season grasses can be fertilized once in the late spring and once during the summer for adequate growth. A medium-maintenance lawn will require more fertilizing. The cool season grasses should be fertilized in the spring and in the fall. Warm season grasses should be fertilized once in the spring, once in mid-summer, and once in the early fall. High-maintenance lawns, no matter whether cool season or warm season grasses, will need to be fertilized once a month during the active growing season.

The Organic Option

Organic fertilizers are made up of animal or plant waste. Manure, milorganite (sludge), compost, seaweed, and rock powders are just a few. Organic fertilizer can be an amazing way to feed your lawn because you're not only feeding the grass; you're feeding the soil. These types of fertilizers encourage the growth of the microorganisms in the soil that get the nutrients into the grass. The nitrogen present in organic matter is water insoluble. It is released slowly so your lawn gets a steady supply of food throughout the growing season. And using organic fertilizer is certainly an earth-friendly way to fertilize your lawn.

There are downsides of organic fertilizers. The level of nitrogen present in organic matter is much lower than in synthetic fertilizers. You have to apply a lot more organic fertilizer to get the needed amounts of nitrogen into your grass. Just think of all of that heavy, bulky (and possibly stinky) fertilizer you'll have to buy. It's more expensive than synthetic fertilizer, too. Finally, the nitrogen in organic fertilizer is temperature sensitive. The soil temperature must be over 50° F to activate the microorganisms in the soil that digest the organic matter and release the nitrogen. So your fertilizer may just be sitting there doing nothing until the weather warms up.

When Your Lawn Needs to Go on a Diet

Too much of a good thing can be bad for your lawn. Bottom line—don't over-feed the lawn. Use your soil test results to know how much of what is needed. Sure, that nice deep green, lush growth looks great, but what about what's going on underneath the scenes? When the leaves of grass grow, the root system needs to be able to support that new growth. An explosive period of foliage growth can actually stunt root growth. The leaves demand more water, so the roots stay closest to the most readily available source of water—near the surface. When you overfertilize, you end up with a shallow root system that won't be able to sustain your grass during the stresses of drought or weather damage.

Your lawn is going to need some help to stay healthy. Get to know your grass—what type of nutrients and how much it needs and when it needs water. With a little time and care, you can keep your lawn in top shape and it'll withstand pretty much anything Mother Nature can throw at it.

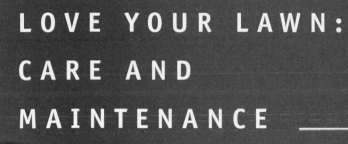

LOVE YOUR LAWN:
CARE AND
MAINTENANCE

6

The Lowdown on the Mowdown

owing is the most time-consuming of your lawn care and maintenance tasks—it is also one of your best allies in developing full, low-weed, actively growing, and good-looking grass. So understanding exactly what happens when you mow will help you think like the grass—and make the most of the hours you spend mowing your big-league lawn.

Picture this: every time you cut a blade of grass, its root system temporarily stops growing, which limits the plant's ability to absorb water and nutrients. The cut also eliminates the food that the (now absent) top bit of the plant provided. The good news is that when a grass plant is cut, it can produce new plants from the crown and stem nodes, causing the plant to become more dense below the cut line. Cutting imperils the plant by limiting its ability to feed itself, but it also gives it the opportunity to replenish, even improve itself.

Mowing is, in short, the good cop and the bad cop in the lawn care ritual. This isn't to say it's dangerous to cut the grass, just that it's important to get the details of the cut just right. There's a careful balance you need to maintain between cutting height and the amount of stress the plant's root system can take.

If you cut too short, you weaken the root system so much you send the plant into a crisis mode. Or if you cut too often, you're putting root system stress on the plant too frequently, which makes it harder for the plant to rejuvenate after each time you mow. And a weak plant is a target for weeds, disease, and drought. We can't have that.

The three parts of your mowing practice include how high, how often, and what happens to the clippings. These are the questions you need to answer to determine your own distinct mowing regimen, based on your conditions and type of grass.

How High?

An easy way to begin thinking about your height requirement is with the One-Third Rule. This rule asserts that you should never cut off more than one third of the grass plant at a mowing. Cutting more than a third of the blade severely shocks the plant and harms its ability to support its own root growth. This is because the roots shut down their own growth process while the leaves and shoots of grass are regrowing. The goal should be to cut just enough to accomplish your aesthetic objectives, while maintaining the balance between blade and root growth.

When in doubt, lean toward long. Why? Taller grass plants are more stress and heat tolerant. A taller canopy allows the soil to retain

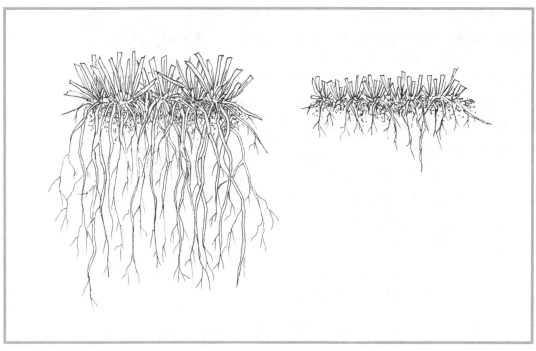

Grass and Cut Grass

more moisture, which decreases the need to water the lawn. Higher cuts of grass can also play an important role in shading the surface of the soil, which reduces weed seed germination, especially that of crabgrass. And if the crabgrass doesn't grow, you don't have to use that herbicide, do you?

The Grass Factor

The how high question can't be completely answered until you consider what species of grass you're talking about. The list below outlines the optimum height ranges for the most common types of grass. Rule of thumb, though: lean toward the low end of the range when the grass is healthy and actively growing. When you're in a really warm or hot spell, or when the lawn is stressed by drought, disease, shade, pests, or traffic, stick to the higher end of the height range.

MOWING HEIGHTS FOR COMMON GRASSES

Bermuda grass *(Cynodon dactylon)*	$1/2$–1 inch
Buffalo grass *(Buchloe dactyloides)*	2–3 inches
Creeping bent grass *(Agrostis stolonifera)*	$1/4$–$3/4$ inch
Fescue, fine *(Festuca rubra)*	$2\frac{1}{2}$–$3\frac{1}{2}$ inches
Fescue, tall *(Festuca arundinacea)*	$2\frac{1}{2}$–$3\frac{1}{2}$ inches
Kentucky bluegrass *(Poa pratensis)*	2–3 inches
Perennial ryegrass *(Lolium perenne)*	2–3 inches

Tricks of the Trade: Infield Strategies

During the 1991–1993 baseball seasons, the Milwaukee Brewers management asked me to let the infield grass grow longer. This was meant for the benefit of the Brewers infielders, including the likes of Robin Yount and Paul Molitor, who were a little older than many of their colleagues at the time. The management wanted to keep the grass longer in order to slow the ball in the infield, giving those guys more time to get to the ball and make a play. As ever, this kind of strategy is a double-edged sword; while it slowed the ball for the infielders, it also slowed the ball for batters, who, on the other side of every inning, would include Yount and Molitor. Yount retired in 1993 and Molitor moved on to the Blue Jays the same year. When younger infielders stepped into their cleats, we took the infield back to the old grass height.

Micro-managing grass height and type isn't at all unusual in the big leagues. When I worked for the California Angels, the outfield featured Bermuda grass kept $1/2$-inch high to keep the ball moving swiftly, and the infield was Kentucky bluegrass kept at 3 inches or so to slow things down in the infield.

David Mellor

When to Mow

In the same way that there are optimum conditions under which your grass will grow, there are also optimum conditions under which you should mow. First off, the last thing you want to do is stick to a rigid, preset schedule. Now this may be not be what you want to hear, knowing how much easier it is to make a date with yourself for every Saturday at 2:00 PM to mow the lawn. But the fact is you need to be prepared to be flexible, mainly because the conditions that determine when you should mow are variables, never quite the same from week to week or month to month.

Your job is to read your lawn, paying close attention to grass height and the One-Third Rule (as discussed above), your lawn's general health, and how much sun and rain you've had (or not). It's really how much your lawn has grown in relation to its optimal height that matters, not the amount of time between mowings. So if your type of grass is best at a height of 2 inches, following the One-Third Rule, you'd cut it when it's reached a height of 3 inches. Or if it's best at 3 inches, cut when it reaches 4½ inches. Do the math on your grass type, and map out your mowings accordingly.

Once you determine your grass species and its optimum height for cutting, take a measure of this height against your shoe and remember where it hits. If the grass is taller than the swoosh on your sneaker (or whatever), it's time to mow.

If your lawn gets away from you—say you've been on vacation or a week of rain and sun has kicked your lawn into rapid growth mode—don't go overboard when getting it back in line. As ever, stick to the One-Third Rule, no matter how long the grass has gotten. So if the turf is 6 inches tall, cut no more than 2 inches, even if your grass's optimum height is 1½ inches. Wait several days, then mow again, using the One-Third Rule, and repeat the process until you've gotten the grass adjusted back to its proper height.

CHAPTER & VERSE

There actually is a best moment of the summer day to mow. Mow in the cool of the early evening, say 6–7:00 PM, when the grass is dry and not stressed by heat and there's still plenty of light. Mowing in the punishing heat of the day is no fun for you and isn't any better for your lawn.

One final caveat: keep the blades on your mower sharp. Dull blades tear the leaves instead of cutting them, which is bad for the plant, leaving it prone to disease, and giving a ragged look to the lawn. Plan to sharpen your blades at least three times a season. Like clockwork.

Get Sharp

If you notice a brownish cast to your lawn the day after you mow, look closely at the grass blades. You'll probably notice they are torn, frayed, or a little stringy. This is a sign that you need to get those mower blades sharpened. If you're using a reel mower, you need to go to your lawn mower shop for a professional sharpening. But if you use a rotary mower, it's pretty simple to do yourself. You'll need these tools: wrench, vise, file, cone level.*

1. Safety first: turn the mower off and disconnect the spark plug before removing the blades.

2. Remove the blade with a wrench, per your owner's manual. Put the blade in a vise and sharpen the beveled edge with a file. Take smooth, even passes at the blade to maintain its proper angle.

3. Set the blade on a cone level to make sure it is balanced. If the blade isn't balanced, file a bit more at the heavy end until you've evened it up.

4. Put the blades back on the mower, correct side up, and tighten the locking nut securely.

---

* You can get an inexpensive and user-friendly cone level at any mower dealership or repair shop.

Mowing Etiquette

Suppertime may be the best time to mow your lawn, but that doesn't mean everyone likes the sound of lawnmowers running when they're trying to relax at the end of a long day, or the whine of blowers when they're trying to sleep in on a Sunday morning. Here are a few dos and don'ts on neighborhood mowing etiquette:

- Some neighborhoods have noise regulations; know and follow them.

- Don't blow your clippings into the street or onto your neighbors' property.

- Make sure your mower is running correctly to minimize noise and air pollution.

You know your neighbors best. A plate of freshly baked cinnamon rolls might help if early Sunday morning is the only time you can find to mow.

How to Mow

The end result of your mowing should be an attractive, evenly cut lawn. It's not hard to do when you follow the tried and true rules of mowing.

1. For safety, remove any debris (stones or sticks) before you begin mowing.

2. Have your blade at the correct height. Check and reset the blade height if necessary.

3. Begin by mowing one pass (header strip) at the ends of your lawn and around trees, gardens, buildings, etc., for ease in turning. Follow the same procedures outlined in making headers for fertilizing.

4. Cut straight rows between the headers.

5. Overlap each row by 2–3 inches to ensure complete coverage.

6. Make gentle turns—lift the mower deck as you turn so that the blades don't keep turning on the grass in the same spot as you maneuver the mower to make the turn.

7. Change your mowing direction every time you mow. Mow at a 45° or 90° angle to the previous time. This keeps tire ruts from developing and helps the grass to grow upright instead of sideways from a constant mow pattern for a more uniform cut.

8. Don't mow when the grass is wet. Clumps of wet grass will stick to the blades and undercarriage and gum up the works. You'll have to stop and clean them off to get an even cut throughout the yard.

9. Always push the mower—don't pull it toward you if you'd like to keep all of your fingers and toes intact. The chance that you might slip with the mower heading straight for you isn't worth the risk.

10. Don't mow in the heat of the day. Your grass will already be suffering from the cut—don't make it suffer any more from the heat *and* the cut.

11. Mow slopes on the diagonal. Mowing horizontally or vertically on a slope increases your chances of taking a tumble with a sharp-bladed mechanical machine. Not a pretty picture.

12. Maintain your equipment. Hose down the blade and the deck after every use and make sure the blades are sharp.

How to Make It Up to Your Lawn after a Too-Close Shave

Repeated low mowing can destroy your lawn so just don't do it. One overly low mowing—and we've all done it once or twice—can set your lawn into a temporary tailspin. Sticking to a regular fertilization regimen over time will help your lawn withstand the stress of the occasional buzzcut. And here's a little lawn first aid: a dose of trace minerals including calcium, manganese, and iron, followed by a thorough and deep morning watering (at least 1/4 inch); then extra water over the next couple of weeks and the grass should make a full recovery.

The Mighty Mowing Machines

When you walk into the store you'll see an endless selection of mowers available. They're all pretty and shiny and each beckons you with the promise of a beautifully cut lawn. They all cut, so what's the right machine for you? Choosing the right mower for your lawn is easy—as long as you're armed with some information before you step into the store. The types of mowers available for the home lawn are rotary mowers and reel mowers. There are advantages and disadvantages to both.

Rotary Mowers

Rotary mowers are the most popular type of mowers for the home lawn. The circular blade rotates at high rates of speed, cutting through thick, dense grass and weeds. They are easy to maintain, not very expensive, and can make quick work of mowing your lawn. They have a large selection of cutting heights and many have mulching capabilities.

Rotary mowers have some drawbacks, too. Most can't cut effectively lower than 1 inch (to get your grass ready for renovation), and they don't cut as cleanly as a reel mower. Even when the blade is sharp, you can end up shredding tough grass, such as Bermuda grass, instead of getting a good, sharp cut. The speed with which the blade rotates can be dangerous. If you don't clear all the debris from the lawn before you mow, those stones and sticks get shot out of the mower and can injure you or bystanders. If you have some uneven grade in your yard, the rotary mower may scalp the grass on the bumps. You'll have to spend the money for an oscillating or floating deck feature on your mower or regrade those areas to prevent scalping.

All rotary mowers are power mowers, but the source of power is up to you. Gas-powered mowers are by far the most popular of the rotary mowers. They're powerful enough to easily handle lawns up to an acre. They're also the loudest and the most expensive models (gas, oil, engine maintenance, etc.). Electric rotary mowers are quieter and less expensive to use than the gas-powered type. They aren't as powerful, but they're lighter and easier to handle. Your mowing range is limited to the length of the cord, so it's best to choose these models for smaller lawns where you're near a power source. Battery-operated rotary mowers are also a quieter choice. They're not as powerful as the gas-powered mowers, but they do not emit any pollutants from the engine, either. Both the electric and battery-operated types are options for an environmentally friendly mower, but are recommended for lawns only up to 5,000 square feet.

The size of the mower you need depends on the size of your lawn. Walk-behind mowers have decks ranging from 18 to 22 inches, while riding mowers have decks up to 54 inches. A smaller walk-behind model is perfect for lawns up to 1 acre. They're easily maneuverable in smaller areas and they can be turned in tighter spaces. Riding mowers are good for mowing areas of more than an acre. They can be tough to turn in smaller lawns, but if you're not physically able to walk behind a mower, a smaller rider mower may be for

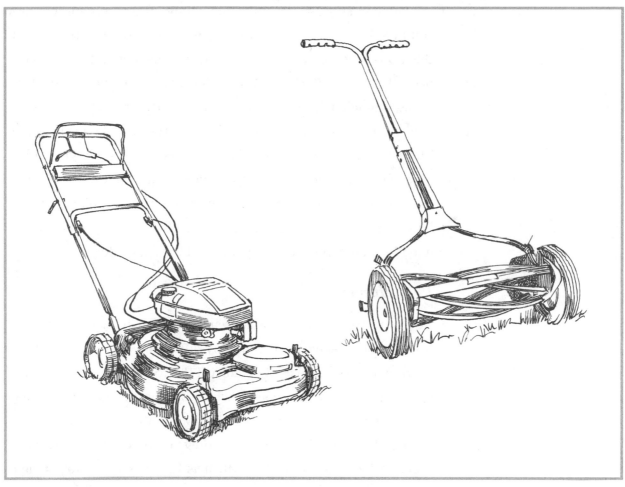

Mowers

you. For the largest mowing jobs, a garden tractor might be the best bet. Prices of mowers go up the larger they get, so choose a mower that's right both for your lawn and your wallet.

Lawn and garden equipment manufacturers have come a long way in developing mowers that provide a clean safe cut and can even help create the patterns I love so much. Simplicity is one manufacturer of home mowers that has included rollers on their free-floating mower deck models for years—I consider this an excellent option for the creative homeowner. There are also terrific walk-behind rotary mowers made by Snapper and Toro that really get the job done.

133

You can choose either a push walk-behind rotary mower or a self-propelled one. The push mowers require you to actually push the mower along. The self-propelled ones have a system that connects the gears to the front or rear wheels to propel the mower along without much help from you. The basic differences are in ease of use and, of course, price. The more features, the higher the price. There is one feature you should never pass up when buying either type of walk-behind mower—*the dead man switch*. Charming name aside, this will automatically stop the blade from spinning when the lever is released by you. It's another added feature, thus another added expense, but well worth the cost for your safety.

Reel Mowers

Reel mowers—both the traditional manual push style and the motorized variety—have a completely different cutting system from rotary mowers. Instead of slicing off the top of the grass with the speed of the blade, the grass is cut using a scissors motion. You may remember these mowers as the heavy, nightmare machines your grandfather used, but thankfully, they've come a long way since then. Easily maneuverable at as light as 16 pounds, they're just right for lawns less than 2,000 square feet. Reel mowers can be adjusted to cut quite low, which is ideal for Bermuda grass or creeping bentgrass. Reel mowers cut grass blades cleaner, protecting against leaf damage, and they conform better to land contours to prevent scalping. The push reel mowers are also environmentally friendly and the only noise you hear is the whir of the blades. You can buy power reel mowers, but they're very expensive for just home use.

Reel mowers—the manual push style— sound good, but they're not for everyone. They won't cut through tough, dense grass or weeds and aren't as effective at cutting heights over 2 inches. You'll also have to use more manpower, so be prepared to get a lot of exercise because it'll take you longer to mow than with a power mower. They're truly best for the smaller lawn.

Tricks of the Trade: Taking Your Lawn into Your Own Hands

I was the golf course superintendent at Augusta for many years and am probably the only one in this business to have overseen the courses of PGA, U.S. Open, and Master's tournaments. Right now, though, I am retired and live in an adult retirement community. Since lawn care is part of our monthly maintenance fee, I have no lawn care responsibilities. Still, with what I know about turf, I want our lawn to look its best, so I sort of keep an eye on the crew as they work around our house. Honestly, I have a hard time understanding the lawn care company's strategy or just plain ignorance. They obviously have professional fertility and weed control programs. Yet they send their staff to cut the lawn with dull mower blades that shred the grass rather than cut it. And they usually cut in the morning, when the grass is wet, leaving clumps of soggy grass all over the lawn. And, of course, they come to cut on Thursday morning whether the grass really needs to be cut or not.

To end this lawn abuse, I have purchased a mower so I can cut my lawn before their arrival. My mower is sharp, I cut the grass when it's dry, and I only cut it when it needs it, never more than one third of the plant at a time. Hard to believe after a lifetime of caring for grounds, I have to rescue my own lawn from the lawn care professionals!

Paul Latshaw

Golf course superintendent and consultant

Edging Excellence

When you're done with the mowing, it's more than likely that you still have some work to do to get that perfectly manicured lawn. This is where edging and trimming come in. Edging actually creates a straight edge of grass where your lawn meets other surfaces, like the driveway. Trimming cuts that pesky grass that hangs around the perimeter of the garage where the mower can't quite reach. To do the right job, you need the right tools.

Edgers

You can choose either a manual or a power edger. A manual edger is just that—powered by you. Manual edgers come in two types—stick or rotary. A stick edger has a half-moon-shaped disk at the end of a long pole that you use to cut down into the turf, effectively slicing off bits of the grass to create a straight edge. A rotary edger has a star-shaped cutter that rotates along between the pavement and the grass to grind up a straight path between the two. Both take some muscle, so you may want to consider a power edger if you don't have the energy to tackle this by hand. The power edgers (whether gas or electric) are set up along the same lines as a rotary edger. A spinning wheel digs down to create that clean edge between

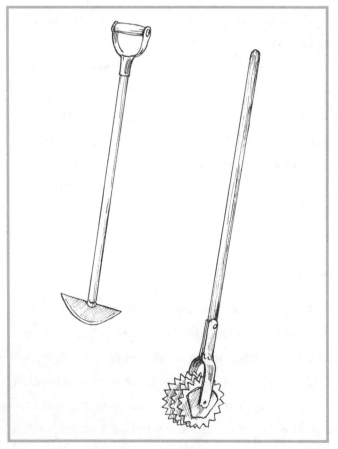

Edgers

pavement and grass. Just remember to wear eye protection as the power edger can kick up debris. If you're an edging fanatic, you'll want a power edger.

No matter what type of tool you use, you may find that you don't have to edge every time you mow your lawn. Some people choose to edge only at the beginning of spring to get a good line that they keep up with a trimmer during the mowing season. If you want that nice military look to your lawn, edge often to keep that grass in line.

Trimmers

Ah—another power tool! Just when you thought it was safe to walk back into the home improvement center, you're faced with yet another round of lawn machines to admire. Trimmers (often called string trimmers) have a length of plastic or metal "string" that rotates at high rates of speed to whack those weeds and annoying leftover grass tufts right into oblivion. Trimmers come in either battery- or gas-powered models. Both are noisy, but nothing beats that big-bug buzz to let you know you're getting your lawn to a state of perfection. The advantage to gas-powered models is that you can go virtually anywhere with your trimmer. They usually require a special mixture of oil and gas to run, so be sure to check the instructions for the correct ratios before you fill it. While electric trimmers are less of a hassle to run—you just plug in and go—you *are* limited to the length of the cord. If you have a large area to cover, a gas-powered model is probably a better choice.

Although we're discussing the work required after you mow, here's a novel thought—trim *before* you mow. The mower will cut up all those remaining clippings as you pass the areas you've already trimmed. If you trim after you cut, you may want to rake up the clippings if they're extra long so they won't keep the sun from reaching your grass. Remember the One-Third Rule when you trim. Don't cut off more than is necessary just because you've got a power tool in

The Drought Drill

During times of drought, you need to pay particular attention to your lawn maintenance. Mow as high as possible to reduce stress on the grass. Water thoroughly, but stretch out the times between waterings as much as you can. And be careful to observe your area's watering restrictions, if any.

Severe drought stress to your lawn is a horrible thing to watch. The grass just keeps getting browner and you can't control it. Go ahead and let it go brown, because believe it or not, there *is* a silver lining to this particular cloud. The grass should come back. After you've spent months of staring at dry, brown grass, a few good soakings of rain ought to bring your grass right back to that lovely, lush green you remember from the spring.

your hands. Trimmers don't have an automatic height adjustment like mowers, so keep an eye on how much you're cutting when you trim. Wear eye protection when you trim, because the trimmer can send up debris. Hold the trimmer at an angle to send the clippings away from you.

You can trim the old-fashioned way—with shears. If you have a small area to trim, go ahead and cut away. There are also handheld battery trimmers that will buzz off the excess grass with the efficiency of a good barber's trimmer. Both are tough on your back and knees since you'll have to get down close to the grass to do the work, but you'll get an up-close view of just what you're doing and you can trim with more precision.

Clean Up

To finish off your perfectly manicured lawn, don't forget the cleanup. Brush off any remaining grass from the driveway, walkways, or patios. You can either use a good old pushbroom to do the job or, if you're *really* a gadget nut, you can invest in a power lawn blower.

Now, these machines are really noisy—so be prepared to get some nasty looks from the neighbors if you're out there at 8 PM blowing away while their baby is trying to sleep. Don't sweep or blow your clippings into the street. Put them back onto your lawn and put those nitrogen-rich clippings to work feeding your lawn.

Tricks of the Trade: Putting Your Mower to Bed

Here are some simple end-of-season maintenance tips to ensure a quick starting engine and a good, clean first mow next spring:

- Allow the engine to run out of gas.

- Wash and thoroughly dry your mower.

- Remove the spark plug and put a tablespoon of oil down the cylinder.

- Clean and lubricate the choke and throttle linkages. And apply grease to fittings.

- Clean off debris from cooling fins with a wooden ice-pop stick.

- Check muffler for corrosion and replace if necessary.

- Scrape dried and hardened grass from underneath the deck.

- Sharpen blade or replace blade if nicks or gouges are too big.

- Replace worn drive belts; tighten any loose belts.

- Touch up areas on the top and underside of the deck with paint to prevent rust or corrosion.

- Remove fully charged battery from rider or tractor and store in a cool, dry place.

Clark Oltman

Consumer Customer Care

The Toro Company

GETTING FANCY:
A SHORT COURSE IN
MOWING PATTERNS

7

Your Lawn Is Your Canvas

That great (or small) expanse of lawn is now whipped into shape. You can admire it as is or you can look at your lawn as a potential work of art. You might think that creating patterns on your lawn is too difficult, but it's not. You create patterns on your lawn all the time—with your footsteps. When you walk on the lawn, the grass gets bent and you're left with the impression of your foot. It's not an especially pretty pattern, but it's a pattern nonetheless. Now, apply that idea to a much neater, more uniform design and you're starting to think like a lawn artist.

To get a notion of how patterning works, you must understand the basics of how a pattern is created. When the grass is bent, a pattern in the grass is formed. When the grass is bent one way, a light stripe appears. When the grass is bent the opposite way, a dark stripe appears. The light reflecting on the bent grass provides the illusion of different color stripes.

Now, try this out. Stand, facing your house, and walk across the lawn. Turn around and walk back. When you look at the lawn from your starting position, the footprints heading toward your house are lighter than the footprints leading back to you. If you were standing in front of your house looking at these same footprints, the light and dark prints would be reversed.

So a pattern is created when the grass is bent a certain way. And your viewpoint affects the appearance of the pattern. Now you know the basic concepts behind making a pattern. Not that hard, is it? So, let's get to the business of how to create a lawn pattern.

Tools

There are two main tools you'll need to make a pattern: a lawn mower and a roller. The mower initiates the pattern by giving you guidelines to follow, and the roller refines and completes the pattern. You don't need a special mower for making patterns; whatever type you use for regular maintenance mowing will work fine.

The roller is the most important tool for making a lawn pattern. You get the basic design from your mower, but the roller is the icing on the cake. Remember, you want to bend the grass in certain directions to make the pattern, and the roller is the tool for this job. You can buy or rent a roller from a garden center—the same type you'd use to roll the soil when you're getting ready to plant grass from scratch. The weight of the roller will bend the grass so you won't have to engage your neighbors to do the 30 feet shuffle to get the desired effect. You'll end up with a nice smooth surface to reflect the sunlight and make your pattern come alive.

The most important feature of a roller is the size. It should be as wide as the cutting elements on your mower. The full width of your mowed row needs to be rolled completely, but with no overlap, to ensure the integrity of the design. Professionals use mowers that have rollers attached, making it easier to create a pattern in one sweep. Unless you've got a lawn tractor with a roller attached, you'll have to use the roller separately to get the pattern definition you want.

There are other tools you can use if you don't have a roller. A drag mat, lawn sweeper, golf green roller, hand roller, or even a squeegee can be used to make the stripes in your pattern. These are a bit more labor intensive, but will also make your pattern stand out in the absence of a standard roller.

> **CHAPTER & VERSE**
>
> Rolling the grass will set the pattern into the lawn. Mowing may have started the pattern, but it's the rolling that will give it that nice crisp design you're looking for.

Technique

There *are* a few secrets to making a lawn pattern. The first is to start with a drawing. Make a sketch of the area you want to pattern, then determine the viewpoint from which your pattern will be seen. For instance, if you're looking for curbside appeal, your pattern will be created so that it will be most vivid closest to the curb. If you want to admire it from your second-story window and don't care what the neighbors will see, you'll develop the pattern with that viewpoint in mind. Now, decide on a pattern. Take into consideration the makeup of your lawn space. A nice rectangular lawn lends itself well to a simple plaid pattern, while a corner yard would show off a diamond-shaped pattern because there are viewpoints from two sides of your lawn. We'll get to some specific pattern designs a bit later.

Once you have your yard sketch, map out the stripes you'll need to create the pattern. You'll want to start and end with the same color stripes (light or dark) to create symmetry in your design. You don't have to pull out the graph paper, but it's important to get a sense of the pattern before you start the mower.

The last trick you'll have to master is mowing a straight line.

Flag Pattern

Don't laugh—it's harder than you might think. Any bump or depression in your lawn can make the wheels of the mower tilt, skewing the line just a bit and knocking it off center. Once you've got a crooked line, all the others that follow will have that same herky-jerky look to them. For the home lawn, it's not necessary to have your lines as military straight as, let's say, the field at Fenway during the World Series (which will happen, I tell you!), but you do want the best presentation you can get. The more crooked your lines, the harder it will be to roll the definition into the pattern.

Start by choosing a straight line to begin your stripes. A straight driveway or walkway will work nicely. Begin your mowing against that straight edge, and you've got a good start to your design. If you don't have a straight edge, you can make one yourself with string. Choose the longest part of your yard, place stakes at either end, and tie off a string between them. Tie the string a few inches from the ground so you don't cut it while you mow. This is where you'll begin to make your straight lines. Mow from one end of the string to the other. Turn around at the end stake and mow the opposite way along

Big and Small Diamond Pattern

the string, overlapping your tire marks from the first pass. Now, you've got a straight beginning to your design.

The easiest way to make sure you keep your lines straight as you mow along is to pick a vantage point and keep your eye on it. If you're constantly looking down at the line you mow, you can lose the perspective of the straight line and veer off without even knowing it. Pick a point, a tree or a window, and keep your eyes on it as you mow toward it. To check out how you're doing, look down and out about 10 feet in front of you to be sure you're overlapping evenly and not missing any areas.

Tricks of the Trade: The Green Canvas

I'll admit to a strong penchant for lawn patterns. You might say I'm known for this affinity. Some favorites I have played with on the fields I have tended include the wavy line (my daughter designed this on paper with crayons), fancy diamonds, and, of course, the "sox" at Fenway Park.

(continued)

Wave Pattern

> For your own "home field," let your imagination run wild. Your grandma is turning 100? Mow a celebratory 100 in your grass for all to see. Cut a jack-o'-lantern pattern for Halloween or a heart for your sweetie on your anniversary. Once you figure out the simple technique of lawn patterns, the lawn's the limit!
>
> David Mellor

Turns

Making turns correctly when you mow is an important step both in protecting your lawn from damage and keeping the integrity of your design. First and foremost, make it a wide, slow turn. You don't want to damage the grass with the tires by making a fast, tight turn. As you approach the turn, mow almost to the end of the line. Stop, back up slowly, and make a wide turn until you're facing the opposite way. Line up your next pass with the previous mow line and continue. The turn marks will be erased when you do the final cleanup pass around the lawn to frame your design.

Ghost and Jack-o'-Lantern

To avoid damaging the grass by going over a mowed section twice while turning, your blades should not be engaged when you're mowing over an area you've already cut. Letting the blades turn continuously over the same spot while turning will damage the grass. When using a walk-behind rotary mower, you'll need to tilt the mower deck up while making the turn. You don't need to tilt it high in the air, but just enough so that the blades aren't touching the grass. If you've got a tractor-type mower, lift your deck up or disengage the blades while turning so you don't mow over the same spot twice.

If you're lucky, you can use a driveway or walkway to make your turns, eliminating any damage to the grass from the blades or tires while turning. Be careful when you do this. Make sure your blades aren't engaged until you're entirely back on the grass after making the turn. The reason for this is twofold. First, you eliminate the possibility of any gravel or debris getting dragged back onto the lawn. Second, you can end up with an uneven cut when the blades move from the hard surface down to the grass, which can mar the appearance of the design you're working so hard to create.

Sox Logo Pattern

Basic Patterns for First-Timers

Simple Stripes

Whenever you mow, you have stripes left behind from the mower—the beginnings of your design. When you want to enhance those stripes, use the roller. Think of a football field with the alternating light and dark stripes denoting each 5-yard increment on the field. Easy as pie.

1. After you mow, roll the grass in the direction that each mowing pass was made. For instance, if you made the first mowing pass *toward* the house, you'll want to roll that stripe *toward* the house, also.

2. The next stripe will be rolled in the opposite direction, and so on, until you've rolled each stripe.

3. The last thing you'll need to do is to mow your cleanup or framing passes around the edges of your lawn to take care of

the turn marks made by both the mower and the roller. You've just made your first design.

4. For added interest, you can mow your lawn on a diagonal and roll every other stripe, as described above. Mow corner to corner instead of from front to back and you've got another easy, interesting lawn design. A diagonal design is especially useful when you've got a slope in the front of your lawn that you'd have to mow on a diagonal anyway.

Checkerboard

The checkerboard design is an easy and popular design often seen on athletic fields. It's easy to do and will make your lawn look terrific.

1. Mow your straight lines across the entire length of your lawn as you normally would when you mow your lawn. One pass one way, the next pass the opposite way, etc.

2. After the first mowing, mow another set of straight lines, perpendicular (at a 90° angle) to your first mow. Alternate the direction of each pass as you did the first time.

3. Now that you have the basic checkerboard design, it's time to highlight the pattern. You're now going to roll the lines in the direction of the *first* mowing. Roll *every other stripe* in the direction that you first mowed.

4. All that's left now is to mow the cleanup pass around the outer edge of your lawn to clear up any marks or stray patches of grass left unmowed when turning.

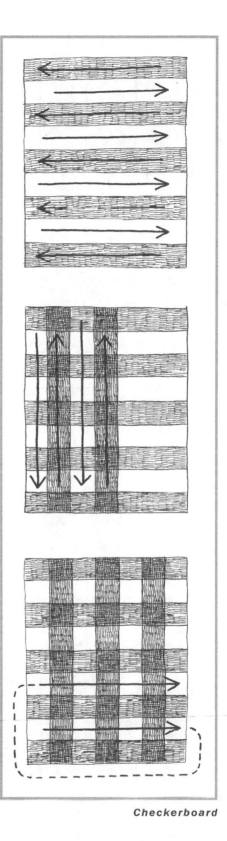

Checkerboard

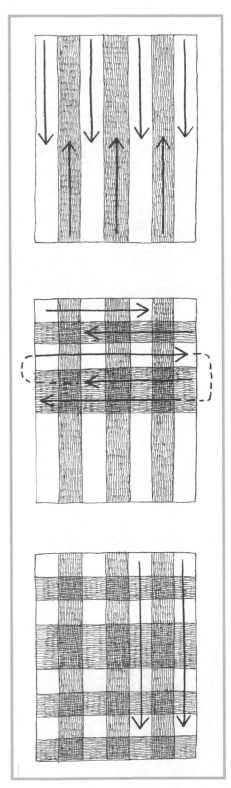

Plaid

Plaid

The plaid design is a variation of the checkerboard. The difference is that you'll be making and highlighting stripes of varying widths to create the pattern.

1. Mow the first portion of the basic checkerboard design (step 1 above).

2. Beginning at a corner and at a 90° angle from your first cut, mow two stripes in opposite directions from each other, ending at the same edge where you began. These are the "thin" stripes in the pattern.

3. Mow the third pass in the opposite direction from the second. Now, return to the beginning edge back over the *second* pass, instead of making a new stripe coming back.

4. Mow the fourth pass in the same direction as the third. You've just created a double-wide stripe to start "thick" stripes in the plaid pattern.

5. Continue mowing two thin stripes, then a wide stripe using the technique in step 3 until you've gone over the whole lawn. End your pattern with two thin stripes to create symmetry to the opposite edge. This is where mapping out your design comes in handy.

6. Now you're going to roll the depth into the design the same way it's done for the checkerboard. Roll every other stripe in the direction you mowed them in the first cut. This will bend the grass in the direction you first mowed, highlighting the striped pattern, but not obliterating the thin and thick plaid stripes made in the second cut.

7. Mow a cleanup pass around the edges of your lawn to create a clean-cut border for your design.

8. The plaid design can be varied once you get some practice in the basic idea of the plaid. For instance, you use the thin and thick line concept in your first cut as well as your second. You'll then roll either the thin or thick lines from your first cut to create the depth in the pattern. You can also vary the design by the width of your lines.

Experiment with triple-thick lines in one direction and double-thick lines in the opposite direction. The variations are endless.

Diamonds

As mentioned earlier, diamonds are particularly attractive on corner lots, since the design will be viewed from more than one angle. Essentially, you're making a plaid pattern, but on the diagonal. This will create the diamond shapes.

1. Begin by mowing your pattern on the diagonal—from corner to corner.

2. Mow one single, thin stripe in the center of the lawn, from one corner of the lawn to the other. Then mow a double-wide thick stripe next to the thin one using the technique in steps 2 to 4 in the plaid pattern. Mow until you've cut to the end of the lawn.

3. Return to the single center stripe mow, and continue on the other side the thin and thick pattern until you've cut the other half of the lawn to complete the first mow. Again, each end of the lawn should end with either a thin or a thick stripe so the pattern is symmetrical.

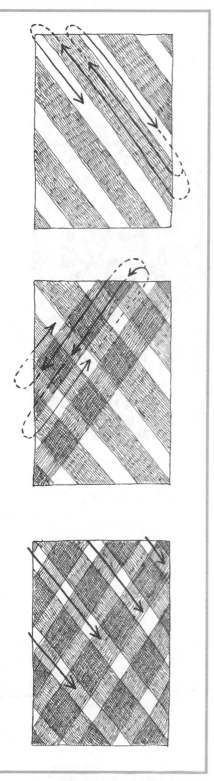

Big and Small Diamonds

4. To create the diamonds, begin by cutting a thin stripe from corner to corner in the opposite direction from your first mow.

5. Continue alternating the thin and thick stripes as in step 2 until you've covered half of the lawn. Return to the center stripe and finish mowing the lawn as you did in step 3.

6. To highlight the diamond pattern, you're going to roll the stripes from the first cut. Roll only the thin stripes from your first cut, following the same direction you mowed. This will bring out the true diamond pattern and make you look like a mowing genius.

7. Finish with the cleanup pass around the edges of the lawn to frame your masterpiece.

Fixing Mistakes

The biggest mistake you'll probably have to fix is a crooked line. It's not the end of the world to make a crooked line—you can fix it easily enough. The first thing is to keep an eye on your lines in the first place. You need to catch the crook in the line early enough so it doesn't spoil the whole shebang. Once you've detected the mistake, go back two lines before it. Remove those two lines, and then the crooked one to reset it straight. You can always reset a string line to get the lines straight again.

In a plaid or diamond pattern, you may end up messing up the count of your thin vs. thick lines. No need to worry—you can erase them easily enough. Your first line of defense is to mow in the opposite direction of the mistake. You'll be bending the grass in the opposite direction, so it will stand up straighter. Mow over that same stripe in the direction it was meant to be, and you're back in business.

Lawn Labyrinths

What *is* a labyrinth? It's a walking path designed for spiritual and personal meditation. The patterns are intended to allow the walkers time for reflection. Labyrinths are created as single paths that you follow to the middle, turn around, and follow the path back to the beginning. Don't knock it til you try it. So, how about trying it in your own backyard?

You can create a labyrinth with the same tools as you would for any other pattern—your mower and a roller. You'll need at least 25 square feet for a good labyrinth. Work out your design on paper first, then walk out your path in the grass, marking the entrance and the center. Following your drawn design, you may want to mark out your path with a marking lime or latex paint before you start mowing. Mow the pattern into the grass, and follow up with the roller to imprint the labyrinth into the lawn. Clear your mind, walk the path, and contemplate your beautiful lawn.

When you've made a mistake with a roller—say you've rolled the wrong stripe—you can erase that, too. However, you can't just roll over it in the opposite direction; you need to get the grass to bend upright with another technique. An easy fix is to take a broom or a leaf rake and gently sweep or rake the grass in the opposite direction to straighten it. You can then just continue as if nothing happened.

These quick fixes are easy because the designs are new to the lawn. If you've had a design in your lawn for a while and you want to change it completely, you'll need to do a bit more work. It's harder to get rid of an existing design because the grass has been in that pattern for a while. The idea is the same—you want to erase the design by bending the grass in the opposite direction from the original pattern. This will straighten up the grass and make it easier for the new pattern to be established.

Using a drag mat or a piece of cyclone fence, you can move across the original pattern in the opposite direction to bend the grass upright again. Pull the drag mat by hand or attach it to a tractor for larger jobs. This process requires slow, steady movements as a hurried job can damage the grass. A lawn leaf sweeper is also a handy tool to erase patterns. The revolving brush can "sweep" away the existing lines when you move it in the opposite direction of the original pattern.

The basic tenet to remember when erasing mistakes is to find the error quickly. Every mistake can compound quickly, from one pass to the next. The sooner you correct a mistake, the less work you'll have to do. Early detection—that's the key.

Tricks of the Trade: Smoothing Your Bloopers

Every time I walk out onto the Major League soccer field I maintain, I see that field as a stage for the action that's going to take place on it. And I like to use patterns to make that stage a little more interesting. Patterns are fun, but they can also be tricky. Here are some tips for avoiding the pitfalls and masking your missteps when creating a pattern in your own yard.

- Use a tightly drawn string line as a guide to follow as you mow. This will help you achieve the all-important straight first line, which is the key to all the others being straight. (Remember: When using any type mower, rotary or reel, it is important to stay at least 6 inches away from your string line. If you get too close, you can get snagged on the string and then you will be spending the next hour cutting string from your blades.)

- If you mow a crooked line, just move over one mower's width and cut another line in the opposite direction. You can use the original line as a guide to straighten out the mistake. The first

(continued)

---

line will show where you got off course and help you correct the second line. When you have the second line straight, backtrack to the first line and use the straight second line as your guide. Now that you've corrected your line you can get back to mowing your pattern.

- If the idea of crooked lines makes you nervous, do what I do and create designs of arcs and circles. That way you don't have to worry about keeping straight lines.

- You can also correct a mistake or just form a better contrast for an intricate design by using a broom or a leaf rake to lay the grass in an opposing direction. The design will really stand out when you make the light and dark areas of the turf contrast this way.

- If you have a bare spot on your field or yard, collect freshly cut grass clippings and spread them over the bare area. These clippings will give the illusion that there is grass in those areas. (This is only a short-term fix, three to six hours tops.)

- If you make a mistake while painting a logo, take a wet towel and remove as much of the paint as possible from the grass. Let the area dry completely, then take a firm bristle broom and scrub lightly over the turf to diminish the appearance of paint.

Darian Dailey
Director of Stadium Grounds
Columbus Crew Stadium
Columbus, Ohio

With a little imagination and some basic techniques, you can turn your lawn into a canvas. Lawn art isn't just for professionals, so go out and dazzle your neighbors with a bit of your newfound creativity.

THIS OLD LAWN:
WHEN IT'S TIME
FOR RENOVATION
AND REPAIR

8

Damage Control: Figuring Out
What's Wrong with Your Lawn

here are lots of things that can make for a sparse, straggly looking lawn. If your lawn isn't up to snuff, here are the top ten reasons why.

1. **Thatch.** Thatch is that brownish layer of organic debris (old stems and rhizomes) that sits between the soil and the grass leaves. Having some thatch on your lawn is good—too much is bad. A healthy lawn will have thatch—it helps hold in moisture and keeps the crown safe from excessive wear. However, a layer of thatch that's ½ inch or more high can actually keep moisture from reaching the roots. It prevents the water from penetrating deeply into the soil, and you end up with a shallow

root system because the only water available is near the top of the soil. Shallow roots equal grass that is susceptible to disease and drought damage.

2. **Weeds.** The bane of every lawn grower's existence, weeds can infest your lawn and take it over or create patches of unsightly chaos that mar the look of your perfect green grass. Those little spots of unhealthy grass are prime candidates for an invasion. Once weeds take hold, all of the surrounding grass plants are at risk.

3. **Disease.** Grass is in danger from disease when it's not at its best. Once a disease is present, it can spread quickly to the other grass plants in the area and leave a path of destruction that upsets the natural beauty of your lawn.

4. **Insects and pests.** That luscious green grass doesn't just look good to you—it's a veritable buffet for all sorts of creatures. A group of grimy grubs or a mass of mining moles can leave your lawn resembling the surface of the moon—barren and with lots of craters.

5. **Wear and tear.** That path the kids take to get to the pool is looking a bit tired. The dog has decided to use your front yard as his personal potty. Grass *will* suffer from excessive use and abuse.

6. **Maintenance.** Whether you inherited a bad lawn from the previous owner or just haven't been able to keep up with the watering and fertilizing, the neglect will show in your lawn. Once your lawn is in disrepair, you've opened the floodgates to all kinds of problems.

7. **Winter injury or drought.** Most times your grass can survive either a cold winter or a hot summer. However, when truly extreme winter or summer weather occurs, your grass may not

be able to handle it. You may end up with some dead grass from severe weather conditions.

8. **Soil compaction.** When the soil is compacted, air, water, and nutrients can't make their way down to the roots. Soil compaction occurs most often in high traffic areas of your lawn.

9. **Poor drainage.** Whether the water flows too quickly through the soil or it sits on top of the soil and hardly drains at all, your lawn can suffer the effects of poor drainage. If you didn't pay attention to the amount of water your lawn gets (or doesn't get) when you water, your lawn could either be too dry or drowning.

10. **Grass variety.** Choosing the wrong grass variety for your lawn's growing conditions (weather, shade, wear, etc.) will almost always guarantee some dead or injured grass.

Thatch Removal and Aeration

If your grass isn't looking particularly healthy, you can easily figure out if thatch is a contributing factor. Dig a small hole (about 3 to 4 inches in diameter) into the soil. When you pull out that plug of grass, examine the layer of thatch between the soil and the leaves. If you've got an excessive buildup, ¾ to 1 inch or more, your grass could be suffering.

Removing thatch isn't a glamorous job, but to save your grass, it could be essential. There are two ways you can do this. First, you can aerate your lawn, which is the easier of the two, or second, you can dethatch it. Aerating involves punching holes in your lawn, through the layer of thatch to create pockets where air, water, and nutrients can once again get to the roots. Dethatching entails removing the thatch altogether (or as much as you can) to accomplish the same purpose as aerating.

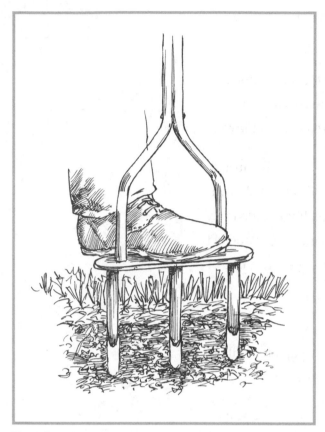

Foot Aerator

If the thatch isn't too thick, from ½ to ¾ inch, try aerating first. Aerating, also called coring, is a process by which you actually poke holes into the grass, through the thatch and down into the soil. Once these openings are created, air and water have a place to enter the soil. The natural microbes in the soil then start to break down the remaining thatch in the lawn and the holes will eventually fill themselves in.

Aerating also helps treating a soil compaction problem. Soil compaction becomes an issue especially in traffic areas, where the constant pressure of foot traffic compresses the soil and makes it difficult for air, water, and nutrients to penetrate. When you notice water running off or puddling in certain areas where there was no problem before, you're probably dealing with soil compaction. You can either aerate just the traffic areas or the whole lawn—especially when thatch is also a problem.

There are many different tools you can use to aerate your lawn. For small areas, the simplest tools to use are ones with solid tines that push holes into the lawn. You can use a hand or foot aerator, which will poke thin holes in your lawn but will take some time to do.

For larger areas, you'll want to use a corer. These hollow tined machines will actually pull out a plug of dirt, creating larger holes for even more air, water, and nutrients to get into the soil. These machines can be rented from a garden center or rental center.

The grass should be moist before you aerate, so the tines can slip more easily into the soil. Don't soak the grass or you'll end up with a muddy mess. The holes should be about 3 to 4 inches apart

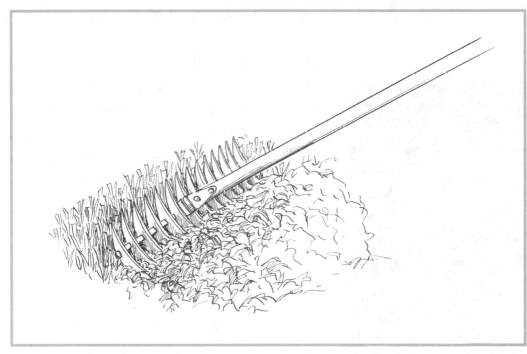

Dethatching Rake

and 3 inches deep. To achieve complete coverage of your lawn, you'll need to aerate in one direction, then do it again at a 90° angle to your first pass. If you've used a solid tine tool, you're pretty much done. When using a corer, you've still got another step. Leave the plugs on the lawn—don't pick them up. Let them dry for a day, then gently rake them to evenly distribute the grass and soil across the lawn. This will help break down the remaining thatch that much faster. Before you aerate, be sure to mark all sprinkler heads, irrigation pipes, or underground cables and work carefully around those areas.

Dethatching involves raking over the thatch by hand or with a machine to break it down so you can remove it. A dethatching cavex rake has sharp, thick blades that cut through the thatch. Using this rake is a lot of work and recommended for smaller areas only. For larger areas, you can rent a gas-powered vertical mower or power rake. These machines have sharp vertical reels that spin and dig through the thatch.

CHAPTER & VERSE

Before you throw in the towel and decide to renovate your whole lawn, give your existing grass a chance to improve. Aerating and dethatching will give your grass the ability to get the most out of watering and fertilizing, and perhaps bring it back to life.

As with aerating, you should dethatch when the grass is moist either from rain or watering. Don't dethatch on saturated grass as the rake or machine will dig up the soil instead of the thatch. Mow your lawn to the lowest recommended height before dethatching and rake up the clippings. Mark all sprinkler heads, irrigation pipes, or underground cables so you can work around these areas carefully. You're going to end up with a lot of debris when you dethatch, so be prepared to bag it and haul it away.

Don't leave any of this debris on the lawn. Once you've raked up and removed all the thatch, fertilize and water the lawn to help it recover from this process. Dethatching is hard on your lawn—think of it as a rough skin scrub— so you'll want to pamper it immediately afterward.

You should always aerate or dethatch your lawn during the height of the growing season, not during a drought or the extreme heat of summer or in late fall. Leaving the holes open for the winter could lead to more winter kill. Both of these processes are tough on your grass, so you want to give them as much opportunity to recover as possible. For warm season grasses, this means working in the spring, for cool season grasses, work in the fall. Water your lawn after either aerating or dethatching to keep the grass from drying out.

Spot Repair

Whether your lawn has been damaged from a bout of disease or from a feisty family dog, spot repair is the simplest solution to getting your lawn back in shape. Areas of dead or severely damaged grass should be fixed both to fight off weed infestation and to make your lawn look better.

Spot repair begins with identifying the cause of the problem. If aerating or dethatching didn't work, you've got to figure out what else is going wrong. In the next few chapters, you'll be introduced to a whole host of weeds, diseases, and pests that could be the culprits. You'll be able to use this information to help determine and

Spot Repair

then treat the problem so it doesn't reoccur after you've fixed the spot. If it's a maintenance problem, step up your lawn maintenance—watering and fertilizing—and see if your lawn doesn't improve. For whatever reason your lawn isn't up to par, knowing how to repair a spot will come in pretty handy.

1. **Start by digging out all of the affected grass.** Be sure to get all of the damaged plants so you won't be battling any weeds or disease after you repair the area. Cut out a square patch—it'll make for a neater patch job and it will be easier to cut a piece of sod to fit a square area.

2. **Water the area well.** If the problem has been a spill (i.e., gasoline or fertilizer) or your dog just had a favorite spot, you'll need to flush it out of the soil before you continue.

167

3. **Level the soil to match the surrounding soil.** If you've had to dig up some soil along with the damaged grass, replace it with some topsoil to bring it up to the level of the adjacent soil. If you're going to use sod, the soil level should be about ½ to 1 inch lower than the surrounding soil.

4. **Just as you would for a brand-new lawn, make sure your soil is in decent shape.** Add compost to give the new grass the nutrients it needs to survive. Work the compost into the soil and then give it a final level and grade. This will help break it up so the new seed or sod will have good contact with the soil.

5. **Now you're ready to get some grass growing in that spot.**

Seeding

Seeding a small area is the same procedure as seeding an entire lawn. Spread the grass at a rate recommended for that grass variety. For small areas, you can seed by hand or use a spreader to ensure even coverage. Gently rake the seed into the soil to ensure good contact and then cover with a light covering of mulch for protection. Apply a starter fertilizer to the area and then water, water, water.

Sodding

Just like seeding, you need to prepare for the new piece of sod as you would if you were sodding the entire lawn. Once the soil is ready, cut a piece of sod to fit the exposed soil with a sharp knife. Lay it down and press it in with the backside of a rake to get good contact with the soil. New sod should sit level with the existing area of grass. And water, water, water.

The areas that you've repaired are going to need some time to become established before you mow them. Sodded areas will be ready to mow in about 10 to 14 days, whereas the new grass from seed may not be ready for a few weeks. Keep traffic on these areas to a minimum to allow the grass time to grow and get a good root system established. Consider roping off the area to prevent accidental damage. And by all means, tell Fido to find some place else to go!

Tricks of the Trade: The White House Lawn

The White House lawn is always green, isn't it? It's not easy to keep it looking lush, though, what with helicopters landing and the press corps trampling and 200 little children scurrying around every year for the annual Easter Egg Roll. Because events at the White House are usually large events held in relatively small areas, our main concern is compaction. After every event, we do a little plug aeration just to break up the packed-down areas. And for long-term preventative maintenance, three times a year—spring, mid-summer, and early fall—we aerate, reseed, and topdress with organic material over the entire 18-plus acre property. But when things get messy—which they can, depending on the event and the number of people attending and the weather—we re-sod. We don't have the luxury of time to reseed and watch the new grass grow. We need to make instant repairs on anywhere from a few yards to a few acres of lawn, so sod is occasionally the only way to go. One event a few years back was held under tents on the lawn on a night rainy enough to float a boat. Shoes were ruined, gowns and tuxes were splashed with mud, and a whole patch of the White House lawn was destroyed. Days later we were back in business, with new sod in place just in time to welcome the next visiting dignitary.

Irvin Williams

Executive Grounds Superintendent

The White House, Washington, D.C.

Overseeding

When your lawn is sparse and straggly, but you don't have a lot of weeds, you'll want to consider overseeding to get a fuller lawn. This method is especially useful in shady areas, where you may not have planted shade-resistant varieties of grass the first time around. Overseeding is also done in warmer climates where you can overseed your warm season grass with cool season grass during the winter to keep a green lawn all year round.

You can't just go out and dump some seed all over the lawn and hope that takes care of the problem. You still have some preparation to do to ensure a truly better-looking lawn.

1. **Pick the best time for overseeding.** You'll want to spread the seed right before the natural growing patterns of that type of grass in your climate are at the highest levels. Overseeding with cool season grasses in cooler zones should be done in the fall. Warm season grasses in warmer areas should be spread in the spring. Overseeding a warm season grass with a cool season grass in warmer climates should also be done in the fall, because you want to encourage grass growth when the regular warm season grass goes dormant for the winter.

2. **Choose the right grass seed.** For problem areas, such as shady spots, pick a grass seed that has good shade tolerance. For overall overseeding, choose a grass variety that is recommended for your area. See chapter 1 for a discussion of different grass varieties.

3. **Mow closely**. Mow that lawn as closely as you can. This is one of those times that almost (but not quite) scalping the lawn will actually help it. You're trying to make the existing area as hospitable to the new seed as possible, so you need to get rid of that tall grass so the seeds can come in contact with actual soil, not other grass plants.

4. **Rake up the clippings.** Excess clippings on the lawn will make it difficult for the new seed to come in contact with the soil. You can keep the clippings to spread as mulch after seeding if you wish.

5. **Rake again.** This second time around will remove any left-over debris and thatch that has accumulated. This vigorous raking will also rough up the soil around the existing grass for better seed-to-soil contact.

6. **If the soil is compacted, now is the time to aerate it.** Since you're doing the whole lawn, you'll probably want to rent a power aerator instead of doing this by hand. Go ahead and leave all the holes and plugs leftover from this process. They'll eventually get filled in and dispersed from mowing.

7. **Sow the seed.** Because you have existing grass to contend with, you'll need to sow the seed at a rate of two to three times the recommended amount for seeding on bare soil. The extra seeds will ensure that more of the grass seed actually comes in contact with the soil and germinates instead of sitting on top of the existing grass. Roll the lawn with a roller or gently rake the area to get the seeds down to the soil.

8. **Fertilize, mulch, and water.** Apply a starter fertilizer to the lawn. Cover the new seeds with a light covering of mulch. Water, water, water.

9. **Mow.** When the new grass plants get to the recommended cutting height, don't be afraid to mow. The soil is already compacted (unlike a brand-new lawn) so the new grass isn't likely to be pulled out by the roots from the mower.

10. **Enjoy your improved lawn.**

The Right Repair Technique for the Job

Do you repair a spot, or do you overseed? The answer is that it varies from area to area. A sparse patch of grass in the shade will do well when over-seeded with a shade-tolerant variety of grass. There's no need to dig up the entire area and reseed. On the other hand, a dead patch of grass from a fertilizer spill will need to be dug up, the soil improved, and then reseeded. The more severe the problem, the more work you'll need to do to correct it.

Complete Overhaul

When your lawn just won't make it in its current shape, there's no alternative but to completely renovate it. Renovation means killing off the existing grass to make way for a new lawn. The soil is usually good and the leveling is fine, but you just need a chance to start over with your grass. It's a drastic step, but it will give you the opportunity to turn misfortune into success.

Plan ahead. Choose the right time to renovate so the new grass will germinate and grow fastest. In cooler climates, renovate in the fall. Warmer climates require that you renovate in the spring. This process isn't done overnight, so be prepared to spend some time to get it right.

Putting the Grass to Sleep

Yes, it is sad, but you're going to have to kill the existing grass to get a good, new lawn. There are several ways you can do this, so plan ahead so you've got the time to do it properly.

You can eliminate the grass by using a nonselective herbicide containing glyphosate. This mean spray will kill any vegetation it comes in contact with. Apply it with a pump sprayer to get it spread evenly across the entire lawn. Follow all manufacturers' instruc-

How to Know When It's Time to Start Over

Here are some key indicators to help you determine if you should save your grass, or go ahead and start over.

1. If your grass is less than 50 percent healthy, green grass, start over.

2. When the soil is good, the grass plants are healthy, and the existing weeds are easy to get rid of, you can bring back the lawn with some tender loving care.

3. If the grass variety isn't suited to your climatic region, it is naturally pale green and course pasture-type grass, or it is repeatedly plagued by insects and disease, you're better off starting over.

4. When the lawn is overrun with weeds that can only be killed by a nonselective herbicide, start again. You'll be killing off a large portion of lawn to get rid of the weeds anyway, so make a fresh start with a healthier lawn.

5. When your lawn is the joke of the neighborhood—worse yet when the neighborhood association fines you for lowering property values.

6. When your in-laws complain.

7. When the local university or extension office wants to use your lawn for a weed ID class.

tions for use and spray on a calm, windless day. This will reduce the chance of the spray drifting to other plants in the yard that you don't want to kill. The herbicide will take about ten days to kill all the existing grass and weeds. Water the lawn three to four days after spraying and, if after ten days you see some grass or weeds struggling to survive, reapply the herbicide until all vegetation has been eliminated. Don't worry about the herbicide affecting your new grass seed, the chemical dissipates fairly quickly and won't harm any new vegetation.

In lieu of herbicides you can use a rototiller to dig the grass and weeds right out of the soil. Even a complete pass or two with the rototiller will leave some plants clinging perilously to life. Water the area and when you see some survivors after a week to ten days, rototill again. You may have to rototill up to three times to be sure all of the existing grass and weeds are gone. It takes more time to do this, but you won't have to use any chemicals on your lawn.

The final way to kill your lawn is time consuming, but will take out any grass or weed present. Cover your lawn with thick dark plastic sheeting and watch the plants wither under its dark presence. Overlap the plastic to cover every inch of lawn and weight it down to keep it securely in place. The plants will love you at first, since you've created the perfect solar heater, and they'll thrive—for a minute. Then comes the ugly part. As spring turns into summer, they begin to suffer from the heat. At the height of summer, they'll start to shrink in the heat and eventually die. It will take a few months to complete this task, but when you remove the plastic, you'll have a lawn as dead as a doornail.

Tricks of the Trade: A Herd of Broncos

Nothing like a fierce football game to ravage your field. Mix a tough game or two with wet weather and repeated wear and you've got a muddy, patchy compacted field. In an ideal world, I'd resod every time the field got hacked up. But there isn't time between games for the sod to take and I can't have loose patches of grass creating a dangerous situation for the players. So instead I have a few simple repair techniques I use during the season, until I have a chance to do longer-term repairs in the early spring. These quick fixes will work just as well in your own yard after a rowdy neighborhood game.

(continued)

1. Rake up debris and loose grass to tidy up the area.

2. Fill divets with soil and seed.

3. Roll the damaged areas to flatten and firm.

You can also use grass clippings to hide particularly unappealing areas, but this cosmetic approach will only last for the few hours the clippings are fresh.

Troy Smith

Denver Broncos

Denver, Colorado

The New Grass

Sow the seed as you would for planting on bare soil. Gently rake the grass into the soil or use a roller to get good seed contact with the soil. Apply a starter fertilizer, work it gently into the soil, cover with mulch, and water regularly. Observe all of the cautions mentioned in chapter 3 to protect your new lawn from damage. Mow when the grass gets high enough—probably at least three weeks after planting—but don't cut off more than one third of the grass to reach the optimum height. You can now sit back and enjoy your new lawn.

A troublesome lawn isn't impossible to fix. Given the choice of fighting with unmanageable grass or repairing or renovating the lawn, the time and effort to fix the problems are well worth it.

THE WEED WAR

9

Knowing the Enemy

**W**hat makes a plant a weed? Only the fact that it's growing where you don't want it to grow. It's out of place. It does not belong. It's an invader on your turf—literally. Before you begin the war on weeds, you have to understand how a weed works so you know how to battle it.

The first thing to understand is that it takes a very special plant to be a weed in your lawn. Most plants (besides grass plants) can't handle mowing— you cut them and they die. If only all weeds were like that, we wouldn't be having this discussion. Unfortunately, there are some hardy varieties that can live and grow just like your grass. If that isn't bad enough, there are also some weeds that grow completely under the radar of your mower—low, mean, and where the blades can't touch them.

Weeds are categorized into groups of plants with similar characteristics. They are sorted by how long they live, what they look like, and their primary growing season. A large part of defeating a weed is in knowing how it operates.

Different weeds have different life cycles. They are classified as annual, biennial, and perennial. Annual weeds live out their lives in one year. They grow, produce seed, and die in one season. The seeds from the plant germinate and grow the next year, continuing the cycle. Annual bluegrass and crabgrass are examples of annual weeds. These annual weeds must be killed *before* they begin growing from seed.

Biennial weeds have a two-year life cycle. Usually, the first year is just the time where the plant itself grows, without much energy spent reproducing. The second year is when the seeds are produced and spread. Some biennial plants my also grow through rhizomes and stolons instead of seeds, so you have to be sure to kill the entire plant to control these weeds. Mallow is an example of a biennial weed.

Perennial weeds live for at least three years, and, unfortunately, they can endure indefinitely if left unchecked. These are the die-hards of the weed family. Perennial weeds may go dormant for some part of the season, but rest assured, they will come back. These stubborn weeds have a bunch of tricks up their leaves to ensure their survival. They're particularly annoying, not only because they live year to year, because they produce seed which helps grow their population. They can also spread vegetatively through rhizomes and stolons, so you have to be sure you've killed the entire plant before it has a chance to go to seed. Even if you break off the top portion of the plant, another can grow from the root left behind. Dandelion, quackgrass, and white clover are all perennial weeds.

Zero Tolerance

We won't tolerate weeds! That's the battle cry heard from lawn growers across the country. Even with meticulous lawn care, those tenacious weeds can creep in. The truth is, you *can* have a healthy lawn even with some weeds. It's all a matter of degree—how many weeds you're willing to live with. I remember when my daughters were young they could spend hours looking for lucky four-leaf clovers and making necklaces from clover blossoms. They reveled in "blow flowers," sending the seed from mature dandelions out into the breeze. I cringed at first but soon realized that these plants are only classified as weeds if they really bother me. As long as it was green, I mowed it and called it the lawn.

Stand back and stare at your lawn for a minute. Chances are that you won't be able to pick out any individual weeds in all the turf. Now, take a close look at your lawn. A really close look. You can see the weeds up close, but in the big lawn picture, you've got a pretty good-looking lawn. Lots of weeds certainly can wreck the beauty of your lawn, but a few here and there aren't the end of the world. Just step up your lawn maintenance program and your healthy grass will eventually choke out the weeds.

Another way to group weeds is by their physical traits. Narrowleaf or grassy weeds look and act like grass. Annual bluegrass, crabgrass, and Bermuda grass (yes, this *is* considered a weed in areas where it wasn't intentionally planted) are all narrowleaf weeds. Broadleaf weeds are any weeds that don't look and act like grass. Dandelions, clover, and chickweed are all broadleaf weeds.

Finally, weeds are also either a cool season plant or a warm season plant, just like turfgrass. The primary growth period of the cool season weed will either be in the spring or fall and in the heat of the summer for a warm season weed.

Good Grass and Regular Maintenance: The Best Weed Warriors

The healthiest plant in the lawn will emerge the survivor in the weed war. There are plenty of ways you can help ensure that your turfgrass is the one that stays on top in the yard. These "cultural controls" are a way to keep weeds in check.

Mowing

As the single most important task in caring for your lawn, mowing can also inhibit weed growth. First, mow at the right height. Keeping your grass on the longer side of its optimal height keeps the soil cooler and actually provides shade that restricts the growth of annual weeds. Mowing the grass too short is just an open invitation for weeds. If weeds have already invaded your lawn, frequent mowing can keep them in line. A weed can't form seedheads when its topmost growth keeps getting lopped off. So, the secret is to mow high and mow often.

Fertilizing

Fertilizing at the correct times of the year is also a key to keeping weeds at bay. Fertilizing at the proper time for your climate and grass type will feed your lawn and not the weeds. Cool season grasses should be fertilized in early spring and late fall when the warm season annual weeds, such as crabgrass, aren't around to benefit from the feeding. If you think that fertilizing your cool season grass in the summer will keep it healthy, think again. The annual weeds will have a field day stealing all that nourishment from the heat-stressed grass. Warm season grasses should be fertilized at the height of their growth period in the summer and avoid feeding in the cooler spring or summer when the weeds are likely to emerge.

Watering

Mature lawns need to be watered deeply, and only when necessary. Those weed seeds hiding out in your lawn, waiting to germinate, don't like those deep, infrequent waterings. Those seeds will grow best when kept just damp with light, frequent watering. To discourage weed seed from becoming established, make sure you water deeply and allow the soil to dry out some before the next watering.

Chemical and Organic Preventatives

Chemical Controls

When the weed population is getting out of control, it may be time to consider using a chemical herbicide to help get rid of them. With the large number of these products available, it's in your best interest to know not only what kind of weeds you've got, but also to be aware of how each herbicide works so you can choose the best one for your situation.

Preemergence Herbicides

These products are for controlling weeds that reproduce by seed. Even if the weed plants are gone, the seed that was dropped is still waiting to germinate the next season. Preemergence herbicides stop the weed seed *before* it can germinate. Therefore, the new plants never get a chance to emerge from the ground when a preemergent herbicide is used. These herbicides have no effect on already existing weeds. You'll have to find alternative methods for getting rid of weed plants that are already there, but you can control the next season's crop.

When to Wage War

Preemergent herbicides only work if they are applied *before* the weed germinates. The herbicide should be applied about two weeks before germination, so determining the right time to apply it can be tricky. So, how do you know when is the right time? Trust the experts. Your local extension office or nearby universities are great sources of this information. Since germination times can vary from even one county to the next, getting information specific to *your* locale is essential.

Postemergence Herbicides

These are the chemical herbicides that kill existing weed plants. These are the herbicides for the here-and-now weed control. There are four different types of postermergence herbicides available. Each has its own method for eradicating the weed plant.

Selective Herbicides. Selective herbicides will kill one kind of weed, but not another. For instance, a selective herbicide formulated to kill dandelions will not kill clover. These herbicides are commonly used in weed-and-feed fertilizer/herbicide products for control of broadleaf weeds.

Nonselective Herbicides. These are the heavy-duty weed killers. These herbicides will kill any plant they come in contact with. A nonselective herbicide will kill weeds, but also turfgrass or garden plants, too, if they're not used with care. So unless you're killing your lawn in order to start over, you don't usually use these directly on your lawn but rather on paths and the like. These herbicides are commonly used to kill off perennial, grassy weeds—a familiar example of this is Roundup.

Tricks of the Trade: The Future of Grass

I think it's safe to say that the future of turfgrass breeding may well be centered around biotechnology. Grasses are being developed right now that are resistant to herbicides, require less mowing, and could require half the water that grass varieties requires today. This sort of biotechnological development is really just speeding up the traditional breeding process. For instance, there is a bluegrass in development now that is low-mow, which is to say it grows at half the rate of standard bluegrass, and is also Roundup resistant. This means that nonselective herbicides like Roundup could be used to kill weeds on a lawn made of this grass, and the grass will not be destroyed by the herbicide. The water conservation implications of growing a grass like this could be tremendous. But don't hop in your car and race to your lawn and garden center to look for this bluegrass seed just yet—because of stringent government regulations and testing requirements, you won't see a product like this on the shelves anytime soon. But it's definitely going to happen.

Wayne Horman

The Scotts Company

Contact Herbicides. Contact herbicides kill only the part of the plant that it touches. For example, if the herbicide is applied to the top of the plant, the leaves will die off, but the roots may survive and continue to grow.

Systemic Herbicides. The active ingredient in these herbicides is actually absorbed by the plant when applied. The plant is killed completely—from leaf to root. Systemic herbicides work slowly, as it takes some time for the plant to absorb and process the poison.

Organic Controls

When you have a concern about the effects of chemical herbicides on the environment, there *are* organic alternatives for getting rid of weeds in your lawn. There are some organic products that are commercially available, but they are few and far between. You can either choose to use the organic products or try out a couple of the following methods for eliminating the weeds.

Corn Gluten Meal

Corn gluten meal is one of the organic herbicides you can fairly easily get your hands on at a garden center, nursery, or online. It works as a preermergence herbicide, mainly to control annual weeds such as crabgrass. The major advantage to using corn gluten is that it is completely harmless to humans, pets, and other vegetation. Using corn gluten meal can reduce crabgrass 50 to 60 percent in the first year and up to 98 percent the second year. Additionally, the use of corn gluten meal can get rid of dandelions completely in about four years. Another big plus for the corn gluten meal choice is that it's also a natural, organic fertilizer. It naturally contains a 10 percent slow-release nitrogen that will feed your lawn as well as ridding it of the weeds. Call it an organic weed-and-feed solution for your lawn.

While all of this sounds terrific, there are some disadvantages to using corn gluten meal as an herbicide. It is more expensive than a chemical herbicide, but you may consider the benefits outweigh the cost difference. Another drawback is that you must time the application carefully. It should be applied four to six weeks before the time the seeds germinate. You're going to have to have a good knowledge of the weed and its growing season to get the timing right. A garden center or your local or county extension office should be able to help you determine the germination time of your weed in your climatic area.

Another organic herbicide is acetic acid—vinegar. While it's the same basic vinegar you have in the pantry, the product sold at a garden center must be labeled as an herbicide for sale as weed control. Some of these products may actually be a mixture of vinegar and

---

CHAPTER & VERSE

Before you go spraying some weed stuff you got at the hardware store all over your lawn, make sure you've got the right product for the right weed. The best policy—identify the weed and then choose the right product for that weed.

lemon juice, instead of straight vinegar. Acetic acid works as a postemergence, nonselective herbicide. It will kill the visible portion of the plant, but may not kill the roots. Since it is nonselective, it can harm the turfgrass surrounding the weed as well. Use acetic acid to kill individual weeds when you want an organic option to a chemical nonselective herbicide. The higher concentrations of acetic acid in these products can be harmful. Follow all manufacturers' instructions for safe application, and take precautions not to inhale the fumes.

Boiling Water

Pour boiling water directly onto the weed. Sounds too simple, right? Well, sometimes the simple ideas can work the best. Boiling water also works as a postemergence, nonselective weed killer. It is especially useful for killing weeds in and around driveways and walkways, to prevent spread to the surrounding turfgrass. Be aware that if it is used to kill weeds in the lawn itself, it can damage the turfgrass as well as the weed. This method of weed control also won't harm people, pets, or the environment—as long as you don't burn yourself in the process.

The Oldest Trick in the Book— Dig 'Em Out

You can use your own two hands or go out and buy one of the many weed-digging tools available at any garden center. Or you can skip the weed-digging tools like I do and use a simple screwdriver. The principle is the same for any pulling or digging method— you want to get as much of the weed out of the ground as possible. Some weeds, such as dandelions, can lose their flowers and leaves with a good pull, but the roots will soon regenerate the plant and it's soon back to haunt you. Your main objective should be to damage the weed as much as you can. Even if you haven't gotten the *entire* root out, you're still on your way to getting rid of the plant. Every time you attack the plant by pulling or digging, you're making that plant work extra hard to regenerate itself. If you continue to work at digging out that plant three or four times, it finally will have no more energy to survive. Once the weed is gone, the grass can fill in that spot. Use a fishtail or a briar hook weeder, which are both readily available at nurseries or home centers. This option is for scattered weed control, unless you're up for spending a couple of weeks (or longer) digging around your lawn.

Tricks of the Trade: New York's Central Park

We have 843 acres of park and 250 acres of turf here in Central Park, so we have to put up with weeds to a certain extent. But our primary lawns—about 30 acres including the Great Lawn, Hecksher ballfield, and Sheep Meadow—are places where we'd rather not see a preponderance of weeds. So what's our general strategy on weed control? Good cultural practices. We mow consistently 2.5 or 2 inches and we keep to a regular mowing schedule. In spring, we mow twice a week and in summer once a week, depending on the weather. We aerate and overseed in the fall, and if time permits in the spring, too. We use a pre-emergence program on the ballfields in spring and postemergence only as needed. We rotate use of playing fields religiously, red flagging them when they are wet or saturated, susceptible to compaction or bald spots. For lawns other than the playing fields we use rotation on a smaller scale.

- What drives me crazy: a truck or other vehicle pulled up on a wet lawn.

- Favorite grass: I play golf, so I'd have to say that a perfectly manicured putting green that lets the ball roll right is my favorite grass.

(continued)

- Favorite grasses at the park: tall fescues or bluegrass on the lawns; bluegrass and rye grass mix on the athletic fields.

- Worst offender weeds: yellow and purple nutsedge and annual bluegrass.

- You have to love grass. It's a passion not a pastime. A lawn will grow, but it takes dedication.

Russell Fredericks

Turf Manager, Central Park Conservancy

Weed Seed Control

When you've got annual weeds that produce seeds (such as dandelions), you can bag the lawn clippings from mowing to prevent the disbursement of the seeds. The weed control factor of bagging may outweigh the fertilizing property of the nitrogen in the clippings if you've got a real weed problem. Dispose of the clippings in an area where the seeds won't be spread onto the lawn.

Top Guns

What's the best herbicide for you? First, it depends on the weed. Different weeds respond to different herbicides. Some can be taken care of with a pre-emergence herbicide—it'll kill the weed seeds before they can germinate and become full-blown weeds. Postemergence herbicides are made to kill certain weeds—after they've become established. The biggest difference between the two is that the preemergence herbicides won't harm your lawn. The postemergence herbicides will not only kill the weeds, they can kill the turfgrass, too, if you're not careful.

Top Ten Weeds and How to Vanquish Them

DANDELIONS—*perennial, broadleaf*

Appearance

Leaves are dark green and scalloped. Yellow flowers emerge that turn into puffy seed heads when the seeds are ready to be released.

Growth

Dandelions have a long taproot (could be up to two feet) and spread by seeds.

Control

Digging out the dandelion just once won't usually kill the plant. You may need to dig out the plant a few times before it won't return. You can also spot treat the plant with a systemic, postemergence herbicide. Cut off seed heads or bag lawn clippings with many seed heads before they release the seed. Dandelions thrive on thin, weak turf so practice regular maintenance to prevent their development.

Dandelion

CRABGRASS—*annual, narrowleaf*

Appearance

Coarse, light green leaves on heavy, thick stems that form a compact circle at ground level.

Growth

Crabgrass spreads by seed.

Control

Good, regular lawn maintenance because crabgrass flourishes on patchy, sparse turf. Do not water lightly during the summer months. Apply a preemergence herbicide in the spring and pull out any plants that grow during the season.

Crabgrass

QUACKGRASS—*perennial, grassy*

Appearance

Light green to blue-green blades with a rough, upper surface.

Growth

Plants spread by rhizomes and reproduce by seeds.

Control

Quackgrass is hard to kill. New growth can occur even when the top of the plant or any part of the rhizome is left intact. Spot treat with a nonselective, postemergence herbicide and repeat the treatment if it returns. A dense turf achieved with good lawn maintenance will deter the growth of quackgrass.

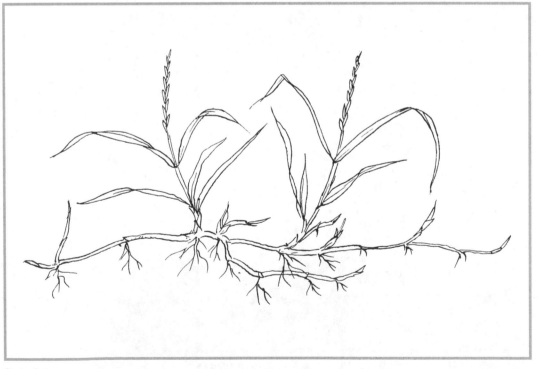

Quackgrass

ANNUAL BLUEGRASS—*annual, narrowleaf*

Appearance

Pale green leaves with small white seedheads that grow on top of the grass. The lawn takes on a whitish cast with the emergence of these seedheads.

Growth

Reproduces by seed. It germinates in the late spring or early fall, but dies out in the summer heat.

Control

Mow high to shade out the seedlings. Annual bluegrass thrives in damp, compacted soil, so aerate the soil to allow more air into the soil and improve drainage. Time waterings so that the surface of the soil has time to dry out. Apply a preemergence herbicide in late summer and early fall to prevent germination.

Annual Bluegrass

WHITE CLOVER—*perennial, broadleaf*

Appearance

White clover has shamrock-shaped leaves with a white or pink ball of a flower. It used to be added to Kentucky bluegrass seed mixes in the 1940s and 1950s, making it one of the most prominent weeds in the northern United States. In the summer, the flowers attract bees, which is hazardous to anyone barefoot on the lawn.

Growth

Clover reproduces by seed and survives with an aggressive above- and below-ground root system. It grows best in moist and phosphorus-laden soils.

Control

You can dig clover up by hand or apply a postemergence herbicide such as a weed-and-feed product specifically formulated to control clover. Spot treat any plant that reappears.

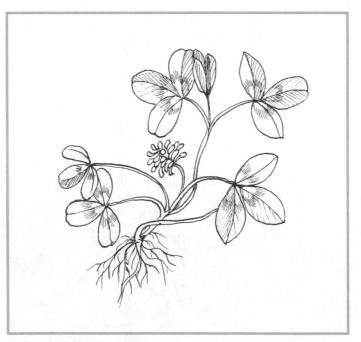

White Clover

MOUSE EAR CHICKWEED—*perennial, broadleaf*

Appearance

Mouse ear chickweed has small, rounded leaves with tiny hairs that make them look fuzzy. Small, white flowers grow in the late spring and early summer.

Growth

A hardy series of short runners keep this low-growing plant alive and actively growing in the spring and early summer. It produces by seed and loves moist, well-watered lawns.

Control

This is one weed that is too low to control by mowing. Applying a postemergence herbicide can be difficult because the tiny hairs on the leaves prevent the herbicide from reaching the leaf itself, so be sure to get good contact with the plant. Apply a selective, postemergence herbicide available specifically for mouse ear chickweed.

Mouse Ear Chickweed

YELLOW NUTSEDGE—*perennial, grassy*

Appearance

Yellow nutsedge looks like grass, but the stems have a triangular shape instead of round. The leaves are also grouped in threes from the stem instead of in twos as on turfgrass. Yellow-brown, branched seedheads appear in summer.

Growth

Yellow nutsedge reproduces by seed and with small, nutlike tubers that attach on the roots. These tubers store food for the plant and are very drought tolerant. This weed thrives on poorly drained, moist soil and is particularly troublesome in low-cut lawns.

Control

Mow high in early summer and avoid overwatering. Improve soil drainage. Hand-pull plants when they're young. Apply a selective herbicide formulated for nutsedge in the late spring or early fall.

Yellow Nutsedge

BROADLEAF PLANTAIN—*perennial, broadleaf*

Appearance

Broadleaf plantain has broad, egg-shaped leaves that are 2 to 10 inches long. The leaves form a central rosette that hugs the ground. Seed stalks grow 4 to 12 inches high above the plant.

Growth

This plant reproduces by seed and grows strong in the spring and fall. The seed stalks appear in early summer through late fall. Broadleaf plantain thrives in moist, compacted soil.

Control

Pull the plants by hand when they're young or dig them up before the seed stalks have a chance to develop. Broadleaf plantain is easily controlled with a selective, postermergence herbicide for broadleaf weeds. Aerate compacted soil and avoid overwatering the lawn to prevent this weed growth.

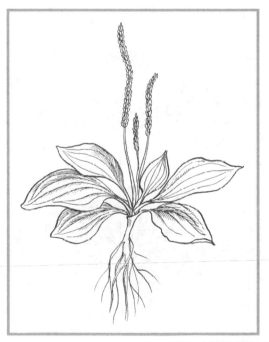

Broadleaf Plantain

197

DALLISGRASS—*perennial, grassy*

Appearance

Dallisgrass has coarse, light green leaves. The sparsely branched seedheads grow on long stems that emerge in a star-shaped pattern from the center of the plant.

Growth

Dallisgrass spreads by seed and rhizomes. The rhizomes can continue to grow after the plant has been pulled up. It grows best in wet, warm areas and high-cut grass. The seeds sprout in early spring and the plant grows vigorously in summer.

Control

Dig up clumps of dallisgrass, making sure to get as many of the short rhizomes as you can. Reseed the area. Spot treat dallisgrass with a postemergence herbicide in early spring or summer. Improve drainage by aerating the soil.

Dallisgrass

CURLY DOCK—*perennial, broadleaf*

Appearance

Curly dock has dark green, lance-shaped leaves that turn reddish-purple around the edges in the summer and fall. It has a tall flower stalk that produces small, green flowers.

Growth

Curly dock spreads by seed. It grows vigorously in spring and fall and flowers in the summer.

Control

Dig out individual plants, getting as much of the root as possible. This may need to be repeated two or three times because the long taproot will regenerate if any pieces remain after digging. Spot treat with a postemergence herbicide. Cut off any seedheads that emerge.

Curly Dock

CHAPTER & VERSE

Use your local extension office to help you identify your weed. They know what kind of weeds grow in your region and can offer advice on how to eliminate them from your lawn.

Tricks of the Trade: The Way of the Weedless

Many years ago, a colleague of mine who was the New England Region Agronomist responded to a complaint about weeds in a customer's lawn. His inspection showed at a glance that the lawn was being cut too short, which allowed it to be overrun with crabgrass. It was also obviously being mowed with a dull mower blade, which was beating the remaining grass blades to death. He tried to explain this to the customer but she became agitated and surly, accusing him of not knowing what he was talking about. Rather than argue, he simply got out a wrench and reset the wheels on her mower so it would cut at the appropriate height. Then he removed the mower blade and calmly advised her that the blade was so dull she could ride it bareback to Boston and back and not hurt her backside. She was stunned to silence, but then laughed, realizing she might have been taking her lawn a *bit* too seriously.

No one wants weeds. But weed seeds are found in most lawn soils and will grow given a chance. So what can you do to prevent them from appearing? Everyone is looking for a quick solution—and they do exist!

First, always mow your lawn at the correct height. Too many homeowners try to keep their lawn cut short like an oriental rug, when they should be aiming for the look of a deep, plush carpet. By mowing high, summer weeds such as crabgrass are less likely to establish in a lawn because they don't have the light they need to thrive. Don't believe me? Look at any lawn that is cut too low and you almost always find they are full of weeds.

Second, mow as often as needed—but do not scalp the lawn. Some homeowners incorrectly think if they mow low they will not have to mow as often. When a lawn is scalped by infrequent mowing it stresses the grass, slowing its recovery, which allows weeds to get a grip in your lawn.

Finally, water your lawn frequently to keep the grass looking good— but not so frequently to encourage the growth of weeds. Light frequent

(continued)

watering makes sense when starting a lawn from seed, but not once a lawn is established. After all, do you want to help weed seeds grow? Watering too much only encourages moisture-loving weeds. So how do you know how much to water? Water only when it is too difficult to press a screwdriver into the surface 2 inches of the soil. To judge the correct amount applied, press your finger into the soil. If muddy water seeps under your fingernail, it's too wet, while a properly watered lawn will leave traces of soil on your fingertip only. Finally, most grasses signal when they need water by turning blue-green. Chronically over-watered lawns turn a pale yellow-green color and become loaded with weeds like nutsedge and crabgrass or dollarweed.

Weeds need an edge to get established in your lawn. It's entirely within your power to give your lawn the edge toward a weedless lawn.

Kirk Hurto, Ph.D.

Vice President—Technical Services

Trugreen ChemLawn

Do's and Don'ts of Chemical Weed Warfare

Do use chemical herbicides with care. Overuse can lead to chemical contamination of water supplies through runoff from your lawn. Use caution when applying chemical herbicides near ponds, lakes, and reservoirs. These herbicides can also kill microorganisms and insects that are beneficial to your turfgrass.

Do follow *all* manufacturers' instructions for application. If you're using a spreader, make sure it's calibrated correctly for that specific herbicide. When using a liquid form, make sure to apply the correct amount. More doesn't mean better— ever— in any case with chemical herbicides.

Do wear protective clothing when using a chemical herbicide. Be ready with long pants, long sleeves, gloves, rubber boots, and a mask. If the instructions say to wear certain protective clothing during the application process, do it. Carefully clean any protective clothing you've worn. Even a small amount of herbicide on the bottom of your boots can track an unwanted path of turfgrass destruction in your walk back to the house.

Do read all the cautions on the product label. Some chemical herbicides are toxic to people, pets, birds, fish, or other vegetation.

Do use the herbicide recommended or specifically formulated for the type of weed you're trying to get rid of. Identify the weed you've got before you apply anything.

Do treat only the areas that need it. If a certain part of your lawn has weeds, treat only that area—not the entire lawn.

Do dispose of any containers that contained chemical herbicides or any excess herbicide properly. Check with your local EPA office for the correct way to dispose of any of these things to prevent an environmental hazard.

Don't apply a spray chemical herbicide in windy conditions. The herbicide may drift to areas with other plants (say, a vegetable garden) that you don't want sprayed. It can also contaminate an area, such as a patio, where bare feet may come in contact with the herbicide.

Don't use a weed-and-feed product when your lawn only needs fertilizer. Overuse of a chemical herbicide can destroy valuable bacteria and insects in the soil.

Don't use any tools or containers that have come in contact with chemical herbicides for any other purpose. Using a contaminated container can kill plants you never intended to kill. Keep all chemical herbicide containers—or any other tools or containers you use with the herbicide—clearly marked and out of reach of children and pets to avoid accidental poisoning.

Weeds can be a pain in the neck but you can get the upper hand. Do your best to keep them from invading in the first place with good maintenance practices. If the weeds do creep in, treat them correctly with herbicide and watch your lawn come back to its weed-free life.

10

How the Pests Get the Best of a Good Lawn

ealthy, lush green grass is the best lawn you can hope for.

Unfortunately, that's what the pests are hoping for, too. It's

like a buffet for the little guys—you grow it, they'll eat it. The good

news is that the healthy lawn you've so carefully cultivated can re-

cover from a little munching now and then, but when the situation

gets out of hand, you'll have to do something about it.

The damage that pests do to your lawn shows in a variety of ways.

The specific pest, whether insect or animal, determines what bad

things happen to your good lawn. Some destroy the grass plant from

the ground up, others from underground, and still others just ran-

domly dig up your lawn searching for a tiny insect morsel to nibble.

Damage to the grass plants themselves can happen in different ways. Some pests actually chew up the leaves and stems, leaving raggedy grass plants that can't survive the damage. Others, such as chinch bugs, suck the juice right out of the blade of grass, leaving it to wither and die. The crown of the plant is a tasty treat for other pests that go chomping through them like a kid at a pie-eating contest. The roots are susceptible to damage from underground insects as well. Insects that feed on the roots destroy the plant's food and water collection center, which essentially shuts the plant down from the source.

Skunks, raccoons, and armadillos cause indirect damage to your lawn. They don't directly chew up the grass. They dig up the turf in search of other pests that feed underground. Ants also cause indirect damage. The anthills aren't only unsightly; they keep out sunlight and destroy the grass underneath them.

The Pest and the Punishment: Coexist, Coax, Control, or Crush

Let's face it. It's impossible for you to have an insect-free lawn. The fact is you *don't want* an insect-free lawn. Many insects and organisms that live in your lawn are beneficial and harmless. Out of the hundreds of insects in your grass, there are only a handful that are going to really bug you. While they're a small group, they can do some big damage. How do you handle these bad bugs? Simply, you need to inspect, identify, and then control.

Inspect

Lawn damage from insects can look a whole lot like other types of problems. Disease or drought-injured grass may have the same appearance as grass damaged by insects. In fact, it can often mask insect damage. A dull lawn mower blade may make the grass appear

Why Can't We Be Friends?

Can't stand the thought of bugs invading your turf? Take a minute and consider this—there are probably hundreds of different kinds of bugs in your lawn right now and you don't even know it. The truth is that many types of insects are actually beneficial to your lawn. These good bugs are there to keep the peace by making snacks of the occasional lawn-eating pest. They're nature's own pest patrol. Besides the good bugs, there are plenty of other bugs that just roam around your lawn minding their own business. These guys don't disturb a single blade of grass. So, what's the lesson here? The bad bugs may get all the press, but the majority of bugs in your lawn are innocent, and maybe even helpful.

browned and chewed, but no tiny teeth have ever actually munched on the blades. So, there's only one way to determine what problem you've got—take a close look at your lawn. Get down on your hands and knees, part the turf with your thumbs, and have an up close and personal encounter with your grass. Use a magnifying glass if you want to get a better view. It may look strange to your neighbors, but saving your lawn is surely worth the odd look or two.

Take a look at the healthy grass plants around the edges of the damaged area to look for insects. The first confirmation you'll have about harmful insects will be physical evidence. Pests feed on live grass, so any bugs you see in the heart of the damaged patches may not be to blame for the damage. Look on the blades of the grass, the crown, and in the thatch layer. If you see a lot of the same type of insects, it's a hint you may have a problem. To see what's happening underground, pull back a piece of turf and check out the dirt. Grubs and other root-loving pests will be clearly visible in the soil.

Another part of the inspection process is to determine how many insects are concentrated in one area. Just because you found

How Much Is Too Much?

A couple of aphids or billbugs hanging around your lawn aren't going to cause you much trouble. The problem is when they signal all their bug buddies and your lawn becomes the local insect luncheonette. Knowing how many pests you've got will determine when it's time to wage war. Your lawn can take a certain amount of bug munching and recover just fine, but an all-out assault can do serious harm. So, don't pull out the big guns for a handful of pests. Make sure you've got enough of an infestation to make using a pesticide worth it.

one or two harmful pests in your examination doesn't mean that your lawn is at risk for damage. There are acceptable levels of insect inhabitation and then there are numbers that indicate a problem. This is called the damage threshold. When you count the number of pests in a square foot, you can determine if they're just a nuisance or a true threat to your lawn.

Identify

The identification of some insects is easy. For instance, when grubs are present, you can actually lift the damaged grass up from the soil. The grubs have eaten the root system, so there's nothing to anchor the grass to the ground. Not to mention that they look like little white croissants with legs underground. Others will require a little more research. Not only do you need to know what kind of pest you've got, you'll need to know when the best time is to control them. A lot of pests only do damage to the lawn during certain cycles in their life or certain times of the year. A sod webworm, for instance, will hide underground during the day, eat grass blades at night, and eventually will turn into a harmless moth. The time to control it is when it's actually feeding on your grass.

Tricks of the Trade: Which Bug Is Bugging You?

It's summer, you're mowing your lawn, and small moths fly up as you mow. The lawn also has irregular brown spots the size of a softball. Because of the little moths, you conclude that you have sod webworm damage, but you could be wrong. This damage may well be the work of billbug larvae, which have eaten out the crowns of the grass plants leaving the dead stems to show up as brown spots. These infestations are often masked when the grass turns brown (dormant) from drought stress.

How do you tell the difference between the dirty work of a sod webworm and a billbug? The Tug Test. Grasp the dead grass stems in the spot and tug on them. If the stems easily break off at the crown of the plant and show evidence that something has tunneled in them, billbug larvae are to blame. For further confirmation, examine the plant crown and roots from which the dead stems were removed. If the crown has been chewed out and has fine sawdust-like material in and around it and among the grass roots, you can confidently conclude that the billbug is the culprit. No other insect leaves such telltale signs.

In my opinion, billbug causes more midsummer damage to northern home lawns than any other insect pest. Check drought-stressed lawns for billbug. And take the Tug Test to identify the true perpetrator in your lawn.

Dr. Harry Niemczyk
Professor Emeritus
The Ohio State University
Wooster, Ohio

Control

The name of the game in pest control is to limit the amount of damage to your lawn. It isn't necessary to crush the whole insect population, but to limit the damage an insect can cause. Some of the methods of control do involve killing the bugs, but others involve deterring the pests from eating up your lawn.

Biological Controls. Biological control of insect pests just means that you're fighting one living organism with another. These organisms occur naturally in your lawn anyway, but your goal is to increase their numbers in your lawn to better fight off the pests. Once their work is done, these organisms return to their naturally occurring levels since there are no more bugs to feed on. New and better types of biological pest controls are continuously being tested and developed for use in the commercial lawn and garden market. They may be more expensive and take a little more time to work than chemical controls, but they are safer for your lawn and your family.

Beneficial nematodes are microorganisms that are natural predators of some common insect pests. The nematodes attack the larvae of such pests as Japanese beetles (white grubs), cutworms, and sod webworms while they're at their most damaging stage. Purchased nematodes are mixed with water, applied to a damp lawn, and left to do their job. Just be sure to check the shelf life of the nematodes and the precise time to apply them to the turf in your area for maximum effectiveness.

Bacillus thuringiensis, or "BT," is a bacterium that kills off Japanese beetle larvae (white grubs), sod webworms, army worms, and cutworms. It is available for purchase at some nurseries and garden centers or can be bought online. When you get it, refrigerate until you're ready to use it—usually up to ten days. Mix it with water and apply the mixture to the lawn with a sprayer. BT usually only works for a few weeks after it is applied to the lawn. It requires frequent applications.

Endophytic fungi are naturally occurring fungi that live within some grasses. As the fungi live and grow within the blades and leaves, they produce natural toxicants and repellents for pests such as chinch bugs, billbugs, and sod worms. Some types of grasses (creeping red fescue, chewings fescue, tall fescues, and ryegrasses) can be inoculated with this beneficial fungi, so as the grass grows, you've got built-in bug toxicant-repellent. Endophytic fungi are only available in grass seed, so look for the word "endophyte" on the grass seed label for varieties of grass containing these fungi.

Botanical Pesticides. Pesticides made from plant material are becoming increasingly popular. The pesticides are less toxic to people and pets than synthetic pesticides, but they can be just as deadly to certain pests. The botanical pesticides break down quickly and must come in contact rapidly with the insect, so they don't have much of an effect on soil-dwelling pests such as grubs. Improved varieties of these pesticides are being researched to improve their residual effect, making them more useful against pests in the soil.

Pyrethrin is a botanical pesticide derived from the chrysanthemum plant. This pesticide is stronger than other botanical or biological controls, in that it will kill not only the pests, but the good bugs as well. It should be used to spot treat areas overrun with sod worms, instead of being used to treat the whole lawn. Purchase pyrethrin at garden centers or nurseries. This pesticide is toxic to fish, so use these products very carefully in areas around ponds, lakes, or rivers.

Neem is an oil extract, which comes from the tropically grown neem tree. It will treat infestations of greenbugs (a type of aphid) and will help repel Japanese beetles. When the Japanese beetles aren't attracted to your yard, they won't lay their eggs in your lawn and create a white grub problem.

Insecticidal Soaps. Insecticidal soaps are derived from the salts of fatty acids. They will kill most soft-bodied pests, such as white grubs, chinch bugs, billbugs, and sod webworms. The soaps work best when mixed and applied with water in a sprayer. They are available at garden centers, nurseries, and home improvement centers. Insecticidal soaps are biodegradable and are nontoxic to people.

Chemical Controls. The market for chemical pesticides is wide and varied, as they are the most commonly used and the quickest way to control pests. That seems like a great deal, until you take into account the harmful effects chemical pesticides can have on your lawn *and* on your family. Chemical pesticides certainly do kill the pests in your lawn, but they will also kill the beneficial organisms that live there. Some of these products are also toxic to people, animals, and birds, so you have to be sure to read the label carefully and keep your kids and the dog off the lawn after applying. Use all chemical pesticides with caution and follow *all* instructions for application, protective clothing, and disposal of containers and leftovers. Keep children and pets away from any stored chemical pesticides. The most common types of these pesticides are:

> **Diazinon (sold as Dazzel or Knox Out)**—used for chinch bugs, cutworms, billbugs, white grubs, and sod webworms.
>
> **Carbaryl (sold as Sevin)**—used for white grubs and billbugs.

The following section will give you a good idea of what some of these pests look like, what damage they cause, and how to handle them. Some bugs only survive in certain areas of the country or feed on particular types of grass. Your local extension office should have a comprehensive catalog of insects in your area and will likely be able to identify one if you bring it in.

CHAPTER & VERSE

When applying a chemical pesticide, heed all the warnings associated with the use of that product. The warning labels are there to keep you, your family, and the pets safe from harm.

The Pest Parade: Top Ten Pests from Ants and Beetles to Skunks and Weevils

WHITE GRUBS

Appearance

White grubs are the larvae of scarab beetles, which include Japanese, June, and May beetles. While the adult insects are different, the grubs at the larvae stage essentially look and act the same. The larvae have C-shaped, white bodies with brown or yellow heads. Fully grown larvae are usually between ½ to ¾ inch long and have three sets of small legs near the head.

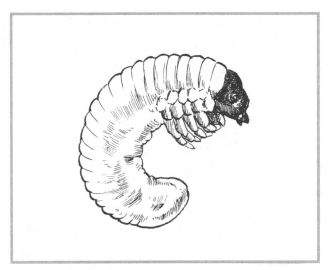

White Grub

Symptoms

The lawn will have irregularly shaped brown patches of turf, generally occurring in the late spring or early fall. The damaged turf will roll back easily from the soil—like peeling up a piece of carpet. You may see skunk and raccoon damage from their foraging for the grubs.

Damage Threshold

Sample lawn before dead grass appears to determine infestation level. Cut and lift a 1-foot-square section of lawn from the edge of the lawn area suspected of having grubs. Stir around the soil to a depth of about 2 inches so you can see all the grubs in the area. If there is an average of six or more grubs per square foot present, it's time for a treatment.

Control

Use beneficial nematodes or carbaryl controlling grubs. Water heavily after application to ensure the pesticide gets through the grass and thatch layer and into the soil.

SOD WEBWORMS

Appearance

Mature sod webworm larvae are ¾ inch long grayish caterpillars with black spots. You'll probably spot the beige adult moths first, as they'll fly up from the lawn as you mow. At night during the spring, you'll see the moths flying in crazy zigzag patterns, dropping their eggs across the lawn. Those eggs will hatch in about two weeks.

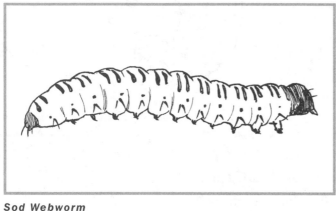

Sod Webworm

Symptoms

Small, irregular patches of damaged grass that are 1 to 2 inches wide in the hottest and driest part of the lawn are a sign of sod webworm damage. The blades of grass will be chewed off just above the thatch layer. At night, take a flashlight to your lawn and you can actually see the sod webworms feeding. During the day, they hide out in silky-white, webbed tunnels (thus, the name) in the layer of thatch.

Damage Threshold

Test for sod webworms with a flush test. Mix two tablespoons of dish detergent (lemon-scented seems to work best) with water and saturate a 2-foot square area of the lawn. In about five minutes, the sod webworms will work themselves up to the surface, irritated by the soap. If there are 15 or more sod webworms to a square foot, treatment is necessary.

Control

BT is the preferred method of biological control of sod webworms, but beneficial nematodes and neem are also effective. Use the botanical control pyrethrum or the chemical pesticides carbaryl or diazinon.

ARMY WORMS

Appearance

Army worms are light tan to brown caterpillars with three yellow, orange, or dark brown stripes down their backs. They can be from ¾ to 2 inches long. The adult moths are tannish-gray and fly at night or on overcast days.

Symptoms

Army worms will leave circular or irregularly shaped patches of chewed-off grass. They'll chew the grass blades off, feeding at night and on overcast days. Large, unchecked infestations can cover an area of 100 miles or more. While it's unlikely, on a smaller scale, a sizeable and eager infestation in your yard could demolish your lawn in just a few days.

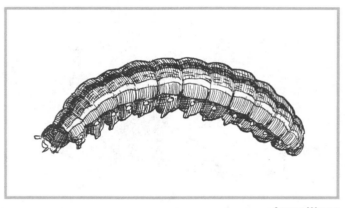

Army Worm

Damage Threshold

Army worms are curled up at the base of the plant during the day and are most active at night, so take a flashlight to your lawn to look for them. More than five caterpillars in a square yard is cause for immediate treatment.

Control

BT is an effective control for army worms, as are neem and pyrethrum. Diazinon liquid may also be used to treat for army worms. Planting or reseeding with grass varieties containing endophytes can repel these pests.

CHINCH BUGS

Appearance

Adult chinch bugs are small—⅕ of an inch long—with black bodies and white wings. There is a distinctive black triangular marking on each of the wings. Young chinch bugs are similar in shape to the adults, but are red with white stripes on their back.

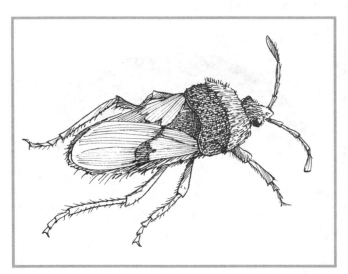

Chinch Bug

Symptoms

Chinch bugs suck the juices out of the stems, crowns, and blades of grass, leaving large, circular patches of yellow to brown damaged turf. They generally are most common in the sunny parts of the lawn.

Damage Threshold

To determine if there are chinch bugs in your yard, push a bottomless coffee can about 2 inches deep into the edge of an affected area of the lawn. Fill the can with warm water. The chinch bugs will float to the top in ten minutes or so. Repeat this test several times in different areas of the lawn. If you estimate (based on the average results of your tests) that there are 15 to 20 chinch bugs per square foot, treatment is warranted.

Control

Insecticidal soaps control chinch bugs effectively, as does diazinon. Eliminate thatch to improve drainage and fertilizer penetration into the soil and plant endophytic grass varieties when possible.

BILLBUGS

Appearance

The adult billbug is a small weevil—a type of beetle. They are ⅛ of an inch long gray to black bugs with long snouts. The larvae, which are responsible for the damage, are white, legless grubs with an orange-brown head.

Symptoms

A noticeable circular dead spot appears when billbug larvae are feeding. The dead grass stems will lift easily away from the plant crown. Sawdustlike debris can be found in the crown and around the roots of the damaged grass plants.

Billbug

Damage Threshold

Use the same testing method for detecting billbug larvae as you would for white grubs. More than one larva per square foot indicates immediate treatment is needed.

Control

Apply neem, carbaryl, or diazinon to control billbugs. Spray the grass and the thatch and water well to get the pesticide into the soil if larvae are feeding on plant roots. Aerate the lawn to control thatch and plant endophytic grass varieties when feasible.

CUTWORMS

Appearance

Cutworms are moth larvae, much like army worms. These caterpillars are plump, brown, black, or gray in color and almost always curl up into a tight circle when disturbed.

Symptoms

It will take a large infestation of cutworms to severely damage a lawn, but you'll find the new grass blades cut off at the soil level when cutworms are feeding.

Damage Threshold

Use the dish detergent test to bring the larvae to the surface. If there are more than ten larvae in a square foot, it's a good idea to treat.

Control

BT is an effective control for cutworms. Carbaryl, diazinon, and pyrethrum applications will also take care of the larvae.

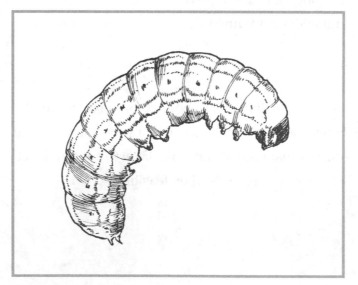

Cutworm

GREENBUGS (APHIDS)

Appearance

Greenbugs are tiny (about $1/16$ of an inch), light green, softbodied, almost transparent insects.

Symptoms

Greenbugs leave rust-colored patches of dead or dying grass, usually in the shadier areas of the lawn. They suck the juice out of the blades of grass, leaving them yellow with dark centers. Toxins are injected into the grass plant as this aphid feeds. These toxins can kill the plant.

Damage Threshold

These insects are not very common; however, if there, they do major damage to your lawn. If aphids are seen on grass blades in patches of yellow to orange grass, treatment should be applied.

Control

Insecticidal soaps work very well to get rid of greenbugs.

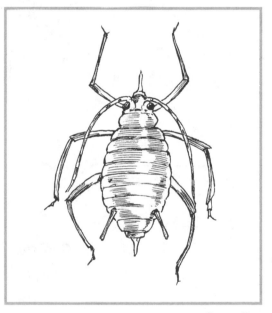

Greenbug

MOLE CRICKETS

Appearance

Mole crickets are similar to common crickets, except they have larger heads and short, fat front legs. They grow to be about 1½ inches long.

Mole Cricket

Symptoms

Mole crickets tunnel near the soil surface, leaving crooked lines of wilted, dying grass. They feed on the grass roots, but the tunneling does the most damage to your lawn. You can even stick your finger into the tunnels, or you'll see the mole crickets themselves on the exposed ground. The lawn will feel spongy when you walk on it.

Damage Threshold

Take a close look at the damaged areas to check for the actual insects. Two or more mole crickets in a square foot of grass means that it's time to treat.

Control

Treat in the spring, when a sampling shows very small (young) mole crickets are present. Apply beneficial nematodes or neem, watering thoroughly to get the pesticide into the soil. Cricket baits are also available specifically for mole crickets and will contain diazinon, or pyrethrum.

FIRE ANTS

Appearance
Fire ants grow to be about a ¼ inch long and are reddish in color.

Symptoms
Large mounds (up to 1 to 2 feet in diameter) of soil appear around the lawn.

Damage Threshold
Not only do fire ant mounds destroy the underlying grass, their bites are also quite painful. Just one mound indicates the need for treatment to save the lawn, but also to keep the environment safe for people and pets.

Control
Saturate the mound itself with diazinon, or insecticidal soap. Treat the surrounding area, about 3 to 4 feet out from the mound.

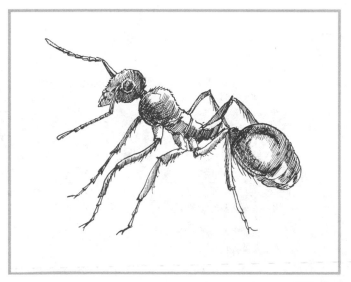

Fire Ant

SKUNKS, RACCOONS, AND ARMADILLOS

Symptoms

Chunks of sod will be pulled back from the soil where these pests have been searching for food.

Damage Threshold

These animals feed at night, so try to catch them in the act to confirm your suspicions. It takes only one animal to create enough damage to require attention because where there's one, rest assured, there are more.

Control

When you get rid of their food source, the animals will no longer deem your yard the local hangout. Rid the lawn of white grubs according to the recommendations made earlier, and the skunks, raccoons, and armadillos will hit the road.

Skunk, Raccoon, and Armadillo

The *Caddyshack* Syndrome

Gophers in your lawn are no laughing matter. They leave raised mounds all over the yard and kill the grass by burrowing underneath and damaging the roots. When you find a gopher mound, dig into it and you'll find his hole. You can stuff a hose down it and try to flush him out, but chances are he's moved on and the water won't reach him anyhow. You'll have better luck with a commercially available trap, but be prepared. You've got to destroy the critter to be rid of him. If that makes you squeamish, hire a professional pest control company to do the dirty work.

Tricks of the Trade: The Scoop on Goose Poop

Every groundskeeper has a story about birds. I had a problem with seagulls in Milwaukee and, like Bill Murray in *Caddyshack*, I had to get pretty creative solving it. By far, though, the biggest complaint, especially among golf course superintendents, is geese. Or to be precise, the goose poop the geese leave behind. How to outsmart these uninvited and overproductive guests on our fields and grounds?

The goal is, of course, not to hurt the geese but to get them to move on. So the trick is to make life unpleasant and/or uncomfortable for them on your field (or lawn). In short, you have to harass them. One golf course superintendent I know spent $4,500 on a very effective goose-chasing dog. This is not an option for everyone, so other techniques are employed.

Noise. On golf courses especially (for obvious reasons) pyrotechnics are occasionally used—big booms to give the geese a big scare, bottle rockets, fireworks, you name it. The neighbors don't always love this technique, but they love the geese even less.

(continued)

Water. Sprinklers, strategically placed, and ideally of the motion-detector variety, are very effective geese dispersers.

Balloons. These will move and snap in the wind and annoy the geese. So will CDs suspended by strings from a scarecrow-style pole.

Decoys. A swan works well—the swan is a sworn enemy of the goose. The familiar owl decoy can work, too, but needs to be big enough and menacing enough to send its message. Even a decoy alligator head floating on a lake or pond can help, though a northern goose might not know what a gator is!

Good old-fashioned ingenuity. My brother Terry lived on a lake in Wisconsin and the geese loved landing on the lake and making their way to the shore and then on up his back lawn, where they left their gifts. He knew that he just needed to make it uncomfortable or impossible to follow their regular pattern. So he installed dowl rods at a variety of intervals across the beach, attached eyehooks to the dowls, and ran fishing line from dowl to dowl. This made the stubby legged geese unable to work their way up to his lawn. After a while, they got tired of trying and moved on to another, less clever victim than my brother.

David Mellor

Keeping Score: Staying on Top of the Pest Problem

A healthy lawn is your best defense against pest damage. You can't keep them out, but a lawn that's in good shape will both enable and show less pest damage and will recover more quickly when the pests are gone. Proper watering, fertilizing, and mowing practices can keep your lawn from becoming infested in the first place. Often, insects like to live in a thick layer of thatch, so aerating your lawn when the thatch gets too thick will discourage these pests. Monitoring your lawn and keeping an eye out for early signs of pest damage will allow you to control the situation before it gets out of hand.

The correct choice of turfgrass for your lawn is another shield against pest damage. It's easier to grow the right kind of grass than it is to battle with a weak lawn that can attract pests. If you have grass that isn't right for your climate, you may wish to renovate it and replace the old grass with a more suitable variety. When choosing grass for a new lawn, select not only the correct type of grass, but look for ones that will naturally repel pests.

THE DISEASE DISASTER

Fungi: The Root of the Problem

Fungi—both beneficial and harmful—are everpresent in your turfgrass. The beneficial fungi help break down thatch that returns nutrients back into the soil. The harmful fungi—pathogens— grow in living organisms. These fungi cause almost all lawn diseases. These pathogens are usually kept in check by both the beneficial fungi and microorganisms that live in your lawn. When certain conditions exist, though, the pathogens spread and overtake your turf, becoming the dreaded lawn disease.

There are three elements that need to be present for the development of a lawn disease:

- a pathogen
- a vulnerable grass plant
- the right conditions.

One or two elements of this equation won't cause a fungal disease to develop—all three must be present. The pathogens already live in your lawn, so they just need a vulnerable plant and favorable conditions to thrive.

Lawn Care and Maintenance Are Your Best Defense

It's easier to prevent a lawn disease than it is to cure one. Improper lawn maintenance is the main cause of lawn disease. Proper lawn care will eliminate two components needed for lawn diseases to grow—a vulnerable plant and the right conditions.

Healthy grass plants mean that the soil and the plant are in sync. If there is a disturbance to this balance, the plant becomes susceptible to all kinds of problems. Often, this imbalance occurs from poor lawn maintenance practices, which create the right conditions for the lawn diseases to flourish.

A well-maintained lawn is all about protection. Keeping lawn diseases from developing at all should be your main goal. In fact, you may be able to control an outbreak of a lawn disease just by altering your lawn care practices.

Mowing

When you mow your grass too short, it weakens the grass plant. Right there, a stressed plant is a vulnerable grass plant. Follow the guidelines for mowing height for your particular type of grass. Mow frequently enough so that you don't cut off more than one third of the grass blade at any time. Keep your mower blades sharp. A dull mower blade leaves ragged ends on the grass—a perfect place for diseases to enter the plant.

Fertilizing

Fertilize only as much as your lawn needs *and* with the right fertilizer. Your soil sample will indicate how much and in what proportions nutrients should be added. Don't ignore this information. Overfertilizing can upset that delicate balance between plant and soil. Too much of a good thing is actually harmful to the grass. It can make the grass grow too quickly where the root growth can't keep up or it adds too many nutrients to the soil that the grass doesn't need. Too much fertilizer applied to some types of grass actually increases the layer of thatch, which weakens the plant by keeping nutrients and water from reaching the soil and roots. Underfertilizing or adding the wrong nutrients also weakens the plant by not providing enough nutrients or the wrong ones completely. Once again, the plant is now vulnerable to disease.

Watering

Many fungal lawn diseases thrive in moist conditions, whether in the soil or on the plant. If the grass is often wet or wet for too long, the door is open for a disease to march on in. Water deeply and infrequently. Water in the morning so that the grass has a chance to dry out during the day. Time your irrigation so that the soil dries between waterings. Aerate compacted soil to improve drainage .

Herbicides, Insecticides, and Fungicides

Improper or excessive use of any of these pesticides can disrupt the natural balance of living organisms in your lawn. For instance, all kinds of microorganisms and insects are destroyed with the application of a pesticide—the beneficial ones as well as the harmful ones. It takes time for a lawn to recover this natural balance after an application of any kind of pesticide. Meanwhile, your grass is at risk for an invading lawn disease. Identify the weed, insect, or disease problem and treat it with the pesticide specifically for that problem. Don't overdo the application—use only as much as you really need to control the problem.

Grass Selection

Choosing the correct grass variety to grow in your area is an essential step in preventing lawn diseases. Grass that is not suited to your climate or growing conditions is going to be weak from the start. A warm season grass in a cool climate or a sun-loving variety of grass planted in the shade is an open invitation to a lawn disease. Select the right varieties of grass for your new lawn, reseed areas of concern (shade), or renovate your lawn completely and plant an appropriate type of grass for the conditions in your yard. Also, try to choose disease-resistant varieties of grass whenever you can. Your local extension office can recommend disease-resistant grass varieties that will grow in your area.

Thatch

Lawn diseases love to live in that spongy layer of thatch. The thicker the thatch, the more water and nutrients sit in that thatch layer than get into the soil. When the plants get weak from lack of water or nutrients, the conditions are right for lawn diseases to thrive. Aerate or rake the lawn to reduce the thatch and avoid overfertilizing that may increase the thatch layer.

Identifying the Lawn Disease

Lawn diseases can be difficult to identify. Drought and pest-damaged grass are often mistaken for diseased grass. Also, many of the diseases and their symptoms look alike, so identifying the specific culprit doesn't usually happen with just a casual inspection. Take some time and have a good, hard look at your lawn.

An Apple a Day—Tricks to Staying Disease Free

Regular maintenance is the "apple a day" defense against lawn disease. Properly maintain your lawn with these lawn chores:

1. Fertilize—fertilize with the right type and amount of fertilizer and at the right times of year. Don't create your own problems by thinking if a little is good a lot must be better. Refer to your soil test recommendations.

2. Mowing—mow when the grass gets to its optimum mowing length. Don't mow too short and don't let the grass grow out of control.

3. Water—regular and proper irrigation is a must to keep disease free. Don't water too much, but just enough to keep the grass healthy. When possible, water in the early morning, not in the evening. Evening watering can create an environment for disease.

4. Aerate and dethatch—keep your soil in shape and your thatch in line. The only way for water and fertilizer to benefit your lawn is if it can actually get down into the soil.

Look for patterns in the damaged grass. Note the shape of the diseased area, the color of the grass in and around the area, and how the damaged grass patches appear throughout the whole lawn. Look at the grass blades themselves and inspect for any color changes, striping, or colored powder clinging to the blade. Lastly, jot down when you first noticed the damage and the weather at the time, as some diseases only appear under certain climatic conditions.

The most accurate way to identify a lawn disease is to get the experts involved. Contact your local or county extension office for instructions on getting a turf sample evaluated for lawn disease identification. They'll test the sample and determine exactly what you're dealing with and offer suggestions about control.

Follow the extension folks' instructions for gathering an appropriate sample and provide any information you've gathered from your own inspection of the lawn. Take the sample directly to the office instead of mailing it. The two or three days it'll take your sample to reach the office in the mail may be just enough time for the fungal pathogen to turn your bagged sample into a slimy, unidentifiable mess.

The Organic and/or Chemical Cures

The best cure for a lawn disease isn't always the quick and easy chemical fix. Applying fungicides when your problem can be corrected by other means can make a weakened lawn even worse. The suggestions in the following section for getting rid of a lawn disease offer cultural controls, such as increasing nitrogen levels, instead of listing specific fungicides for each disease. The world of chemical fungicides is changing constantly and some new biological controls and products are being tested for use on the home lawn. This makes it difficult to accurately state exactly what chemical is appropriate for what disease. The basic rule of thumb is any time you decide to apply a fungicide, be sure you've correctly and precisely identified the disease and that you purchase and use a fungicide specifically formulated to control that disease.

Blight and Molds, Smuts and Patches:
Top Ten Lawn Diseases and How to Spot Them

BROWN PATCH

Appearance

Brown patch appears as circular patches of brown grass, ranging in size from a few inches to several feet in diameter. The leaf tips brown and you'll see lesions on the blades. When the grass is cut short, the outer edges of the patch may develop a bluish tint called the smoke ring. During humid weather,

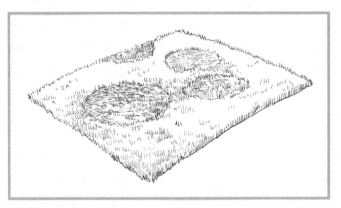

Brown Patch

the grass inside the patch of the smoke ring may recover after two to three weeks, leaving a brown ring of dead grass around an inner patch of green grass.

The Right Conditions

Brown patch forms in the summer during hot, humid weather. This disease can infect any type of grass, but tall fescue, perennial ryegrass, St. Augustine grass, and centipede grass are particularly susceptible. Brown patch occurs mainly when the temperature is 85° F or above during the day and 65° F or above at night. Excessive moisture from dew and irrigation helps this disease thrive.

Control

Allow the grass to dry between watering. Water deeply and infrequently early in the morning. Avoid late-evening watering, especially when the temperature during the night is going to be 65° F or higher. Aerate the lawn to reduce thatch and avoid excessive application of nitrogen-rich fertilizer. The heaviest application of fertilizer for cool season grasses should be in the fall and for warm season grasses in the spring. If brown patch develops in shady areas, prune trees or foliage to allow in sunlight and increase air circulation to help dry out the grass.

DOLLAR SPOT

Appearance

Patches of dollar spot are small (1 to 5 inches in diameter) dead spots in the lawn that may grow together to create larger diseased areas. These spots contain bleached, straw-colored grass. Hourglass-shaped blotches appear on the blades, and white, cottony threads of fungus are visible on the plant in the morning.

The Right Conditions

Lawns are most susceptible to dollar spot during the warm days and cool nights in the spring and fall. Lawns with heavy thatch, wet grass, and a nitrogen deficiency are most vulnerable. This disease is most problematic on Kentucky bluegrass and bentgrass, but other grass types may be affected.

Control

Aerate to reduce thatch and fertilize to increase the level of nitrogen. Water when necessary, but allow the grass to dry out between waterings. Reseed or plant with a disease-resistant grass variety.

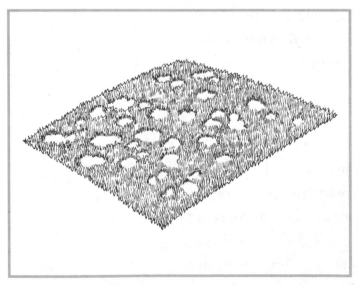

Dollar Spot on the Lawn

Dollar Spot on the Grass Plant

LEAF SPOT

Appearance

The most obvious sign of leaf spot is elongated, circular spots on the grass blades. These spots have a brown center with black to purple edges.

The Right Conditions

Leaf spot is most severe during overcast, cool, wet weather. Lawns that are mowed too short or improperly watered are most vulnerable. Kentucky bluegrass, fescue, and Bermuda grass lawns are most prone to leaf spot.

Control

Adjust mowing height to the higher end of the recommended height for your grass. Cut back on watering until weather conditions improve and avoid a heavy nitrogen-based fertilization. Several grass varieties are available that are resistant to leaf spot, so consider the investment to plant one of these varieties.

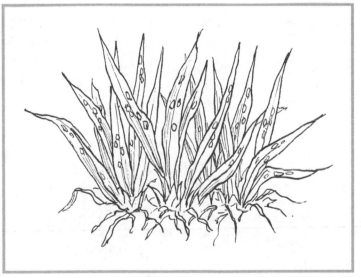

Leaf Spot

SNOW MOLDS

Appearance

There are two types of snow molds—pink and gray. Both snow molds appear as patches of dead grass, which show up after the snow cover melts. Areas affected with pink snow mold have a pinkish mold around the edges, while gray snow mold spots have a grayish-brown fuzzy mold surrounding the dead spot.

The Right Conditions

Snow molds occur only in areas that receive snow and most often when the snow cover is on the ground for several months. These molds thrive in cooler, moist conditions that receive little light—under the snow is a perfect habitat.

Control

Avoid excessive nitrogen applications in the fall. Mow until the grass stops growing in the fall because longer grass under the snow is more susceptible to snow molds. Aerate and reduce thatch to improve drainage.

POWDERY MILDEW

Appearance

This disease appears as a white or grayish powdery substance on the upper growth of the plant. The grass often looks like it has been dusted with flour.

The Right Conditions

While all grasses can develop powdery mildew, Kentucky bluegrass is especially susceptible. It will grow in areas of the lawn without much air circulation and sunlight, especially shady areas. The high humidity and warm temperatures of summer are perfect conditions for powdery mildew.

Control

Improve air circulation and increase sunlight by pruning trees and shrubs. Choose a shade-tolerant variety of grass to plant in vulnerable areas. Avoid overwatering and overfertilizing in shady areas of the lawn.

RUST

Appearance

Rust begins as small, yellow spots on leaves that develop into rust-colored patches of spores. The entire affected area takes on a rust-colored cast.

The Right Conditions

Any stressed grass can be overtaken by rust, but Kentucky bluegrass, ryegrass, and zoysia grass lawns are most likely to develop it. Moderately warm, moist weather and periods when dew stays on the grass for 10 to 12 hours a day are the perfect conditions for rust to grow.

Control

Rust doesn't stand a chance on a properly maintained lawn. When rust pops up in the lawn, continue to follow your fertilization program to stimulate grass growth. The grass will grow out the rust. Mow higher and more frequently during this growth period.

RED THREAD

Appearance

Patches of grass with red thread will turn brown and tangles of red, threadlike patches of fungus appear at the leaf ends. The entire affected area will take on a reddish tinge.

The Right Conditions

Red thread grows during periods of cool, moist weather. Lawns of fine fescue and perennial ryegrass are most susceptible, but Kentucky bluegrass, bentgrass, and Bermuda grass may also develop this disease. Poorly fertilized lawns are ripe for red thread.

Control

Maintain properly balanced nitrogen levels and pH with your fertilization program.

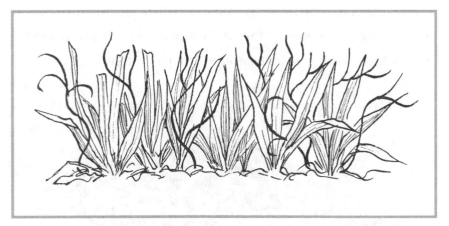

Red Thread

FUSARIUM BLIGHT

Appearance

Fusarium blight begins as scattered, small circular spots of dead grass. The grass turns a dull tan to a reddish brown. As the patches enlarge, live green grass starts to grow back in the center of the patch, creating classic *frog eye* patterns in the lawn.

The Right Conditions

This disease emerges in hot, dry, windy weather. Drought-stressed Kentucky bluegrass is especially susceptible, although perennial ryegrass, bentgrass, and tall fescue may also be affected. Turf with shallow root systems from incorrect watering is an invitation for fusarium blight.

Control

Aerate the lawn to control thatch. Improve watering practices and apply a light nitrogen fertilizer. Water deeply to ensure the moisture reaches the root system. Mow at the correct height and reseed or plant with disease-resistant varieties when possible.

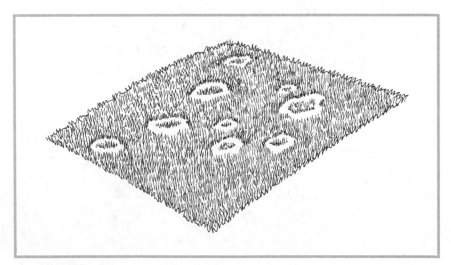

Fusarium Blight

PYTHIUM BLIGHT

Appearance

Pythium blight, also known as grease spot, causes small areas of grass to turn light to reddish brown and die. These areas often look water soaked or slimy when wet. A white, cottony fungus can be seen on the blades of damaged grass in the early morning.

The Right Conditions

This disease is problematic in warm, humid weather. Lawns with a high soil pH are more susceptible. Pythium blight is easily carried throughout the lawn by equipment or water runoff. Development of the disease on the lawn will often follow mowing patterns or patterns of water runoff.

Control

Aerate to reduce thatch and increase water penetration. Test the soil and correct any alkalinity imbalance. Water in the morning and avoid mowing wet grass.

STRIPE SMUT

Appearance

Stripe smut turns grass blades pale green to yellow. Masses of spores form a stripe on the blade, turning gray to black. The leaves curl, appear shredded at the ends, and die. Grass in diseased areas grows slower than the surrounding healthy grass.

The Right Conditions

Stripe smut is most active in the cooler weather of spring and fall. The damaged plants die in the summer, but the heat of the summer effectively controls the spread of the disease.

Control

Avoid overwatering and follow a regular fertilization program. Reduce excessive thatch buildup.

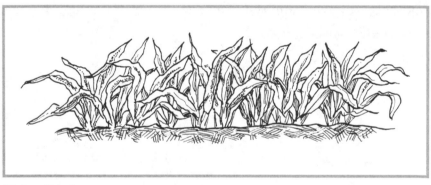

Stripe Smut

A lawn disease isn't the end of the world for your grass. While you're surely better off preventing the whole scenario with proper lawn maintenance, knowing what to do when a disease moves in can prove invaluable.

LIVING IT UP WITH YOUR LAWN

12

The Crosstown Rivalry of Lawn and Garden

Who's to say what is the perfect landscape? After all, a lawn is just a whole bunch of grass plants growing together, so technically it's a sort of garden. For you lawnatics, your lawn is just one big garden and as far as you're concerned, your landscaping is all set. For other people, the whole idea of a landscape is a mixture of all kinds of plants, trees, shrubs, and grass laid out to make a harmonious blend of nature. How much lawn versus how much garden? It's a longtime debate faced by homeowners all over the world. Of course, personal preference plays an important role, but there are some things you might consider when deciding how to divide the yard between lawn and garden.

Featherreed Grass

Water is a natural resource that's always in demand. In some areas of the country it takes constant irrigation to maintain a lawn, so reducing lawn size is becoming a trendy way to make a statement about water conservation. Generally, it takes much less water to maintain a garden or a tree than it does to keep a lawn thriving. Other kinds of plants can withstand water conservation practices—such as heavy mulching—that turfgrass can't. Reducing the amount of grass in your yard and replacing it with other types of plants can and will save water. Extending your garden beds out a few feet is a simple way to reduce the lawn size without a drastic change in how your lawn fits into your landscape.

If you want to take it one step farther, think about placing a garden in the middle of the lawn. Plot out the size and shape of the area with a length of rope. Carefully dig up the sod, keeping the edges as clean as you can. If the sod is healthy, recycle it by using it to replace bare spots in other areas of the lawn (see chapter 8 for spot repair instructions). Amend the soil with compost or other materials to provide a healthy environment for the new plants and plant away. Place mulch around the plantings to help conserve moisture. Edge the area with plastic edging or fencing to protect it from mower and trimmer damage.

There is a way to get the best of both worlds—ornamental grasses. The beauty of ornamental grasses is in the foliage. The variations on the leaves and flowers are endless. These plants have the same growth habits and climatic requirements as turfgrass. Varieties are separated into either cool season or warm season ornamental grasses, just like turfgrass. Ornamental grasses grow either in clumps or by spreading rhizomes. The clumping varieties are popular as they fit nicely into garden beds and don't invade the surrounding plants.

Spreading varieties are often used in areas where you want some broad coverage, such as the far edges of the lawn, since they spread vigorously and can take over the surrounding plants if not kept under control.

Plant ornamental grasses as you would any other plant. In general, ornamental grasses should be planted in the spring (for both cool season and warm season varieties) so the plant has a chance to get a good root system in place before any extreme weather. Work a slow-release 10–10–10 garden fertilizer into the soil before planting and you should be all set because ornamental grasses don't require much fertilization after planting. Adding too much nitrogen will cause the plants to grow rapidly just like turfgrass, so keep any additional fertilization to a minimum. These grasses are quite drought resistant, but can

Indian Grass

always benefit from a layer of mulch to help retain any moisture that's available. They may go dormant during times of drought, but will come right back after a good soaking rain. Prune the foliage in the spring before the growing season and use the distinctive dried leaves and flowers to make something pretty.

Ornamental grass varieties have their own particular growth habits, so check with the nursery to be sure that the type you choose is right for the area you have in mind. Some types of cool season ornamental grasses you might choose are blue fescue, blue lyme-grass, featherreed grass, and northern sea oats. Various warm season grasses include indian grass, moor grass, fountain grass, and ribbon grass.

How much lawn should you actually try to manage? Smaller-sized lots have many homeowners and gardeners rethinking the amount of lawn they need to enjoy the yard. The beauty of a yard is

Wood Chip Path

that you can change the landscape from garden to lawn or from lawn to garden in one growing season. You can even change it back again the next year. The needs you have for lawn space may change over time, so just remember, nothing is permanent when it comes to lawn and garden space.

Paths

Getting from one spot in the yard to the other can wear down your lawn. Just think of the worn-out patches from the house to the garden or from the garage to the shed. Every wheelbarrow or garbage can that is dragged across the same patch of lawn is bound to do some damage. Not only does the grass itself get beat on every time you make that trek, but the soil gets compacted from the constant weight applied in the same area. That's a formula for a weak and spotty patch of lawn.

Stone Path

Consider making a path to cut down on the wear and tear on your lawn. There are so many different types of materials available—from simple mulch to elaborate tiles and stones—that a path can be anything you want it to be. The purpose of a path is to get you from one place to another, so take a look around the yard and see where the natural paths are being created in the grass. If you don't want a direct route through the center of your yard, create a meandering pathway around the edges of gardens or along the side of the house to reduce traffic areas through the lawn. A path is a natural invitation to have people step where you want them to.

Paths can be created in many ways. Here are some suggestions:

Mulch—probably the easiest way to establish a path other than to leave bare grass. Mark off the area you want as a path, cover the area with a thick, dark plastic, and then cover it with mulch. Consider installing a barrier on the edges of the path to keep the mulch in, such as one you'd use around a garden. This method is not

Pay the Price for Snow and Ice

Like any homeowner who suffers the perils of icy, snowy winters, you're inclined to keep salt at the ready for keeping driveways and sidewalks from getting too treacherous. Next time you're stocking up for winter, though, read the label of your ice-melt product before you buy and think about the damage it might do to your grass through the inevitable runoff. First off, do not buy sodium chloride (salt) to de-ice your surfaces. The salt will certainly seep into your lawn edges and kill it. Reach instead for a product whose active ingredient is potassium chloride, or better yet, calcium chloride. Calcium chloride–based products are the most grass friendly, pet friendly, and pavement friendly available. They cost a little more than salt, but they're worth it in the damage you *don't* do to your grass and other surfaces.

recommended for high-traffic areas because mulch can jump barriers and create a mess on the lawn. Mulch also has a tendency to become thin in spots over time, so you'll need to fill in those areas as needed.

Stone—you can use either loose stones or stones set in mortar. A loose stone path should be contained by a barrier to prevent stones from getting spread into the lawn where they can damage your mower. Loose stones aren't all that stable and not a good idea for areas where you'll need to wheel machinery back and forth. A set stone path is more permanent and stable and can handle both foot and machine traffic.

Tiles—whether decorative or utilitarian, tiles are becoming more popular for use in pathways. You can go wild with the decorative tiles available at many home improvement and garden centers and create a myriad of designs in your path. These paths are stable and fine for both people and machines. If the tiles aren't set in mortar, watch for any shifting or heaving as one-half-inch difference in height from one tile to the next could mean an nasty fall for a unsuspecting person.

Concrete—a concrete pathway is very durable and can stand up to just about any kind of traffic. Use this for any areas where you lug heavy equipment and you'll have a nice smooth walkway to use. Concrete pathways are pretty permanent structures, so be sure you've mapped out a good path that you can stand looking at for a long time.

Playspots

What's more fun than you and your kids out enjoying the yard? Nothing, however, the area constantly in use is going to suffer some damage. Whether it's a swing set or general play, there are some ways you can lessen the damage to your lawn surrounding these playspots.

1. Take care of the grass. Water properly to keep the blades supple so they won't break off under the kids' feet.

2. Mow high to reduce the chances of other types of stress on the grass—drought, insects, weeds, and disease.

3. Use hardy types of grass that can withstand the traffic. See chapter 1 for the discussion on grass types.

4. Designate an area for toy storage. Objects left on the lawn prevent sun and water from getting to the grass and can potentially damage the area. Even with the storage area, check the lawn for toys before you mow. Don't damage your mower by accidentally running over a small toy—your blades are worth the couple of minutes it takes for a toy sweep.

Finally, the area that'll take the most abuse will be around the swing set. The grass under a swing set isn't going to survive with all of the traffic of those little feet, so consider placing some sand underneath the swings to cover up that bare patch of yard. The sand will also help protect against the extreme soil compaction that occurs after so much traffic in one particular area. If too much sand escapes into the surrounding turf, you can suck it right up with an industrial vacuum (such as a wet/dry shop vacuum) and just deposit the sand right back where you want it.

A Word Against Slip-'N-Slide

What would you have without this Great American institution? Well, a better lawn for one thing. Think about how the Slip-'N-Slide works—a long plastic mat is rolled out onto the lawn, it's wet down with a constant stream of water from the hose, then slid on by kids of all ages and sizes. Let's break this down into its most basic lawn-damaging parts.

1. The plastic mat. This will keep any sun from reaching the grass underneath. Unless the kids remember to roll up the mat as soon as they're done, you've got a grass-killing shade that'll leave a nasty stripe of brown grass.

2. The water. Turn on the hose and let the water flow—down the mat and all over your lawn. This is a dangerous overwatering situation. The water doesn't stay on the mat—it floods your lawn in the area for as long as the hose is on.

3. The kids. Never mind the weight of the kids sliding across the lawn on the mat, imagine all those feet running from one end of the mat to the other. On soggy grass. With no regard for your tender lawn. This is not normal wear—it's downright lawn abuse.

So what's the solution? Let the kids use the Slip-'N-Slide at the neighbor's house.

Parties

Damage control is the name of the game when protecting your lawn during those outdoor parties. Remember—the best defense for your lawn is a good offense. Keep your lawn in terrific shape throughout the year and you won't have to worry about the grass rebounding from an occasion or two of heavy use. A properly cared for lawn is one that can take the abuse, but bounce back once things get back to normal. All the talk in the preceding chapters— from choosing the right grass to a proper maintenance program—has led you up to the point of having a lawn that others want to enjoy also.

> **CHAPTER & VERSE**
>
> Don't sweat the small stuff. In the scheme of things, a party or two isn't that detrimental to your lawn. In the life of your lawn, you're going to have times where it gets trampled a bit more than usual. Don't worry—your grass can take it.

Tricks of the Trade: Stones on Your Grass

It would be nice if all I had to worry about was keeping my grass green for home Patriots games. But any professional sports field groundskeeper will tell you it's never that simple.

The New England Patriots finally made fans' dreams come true when they moved into a new stadium for the 2002 season. It's a great stadium and I had the privilege of building the field to my exact specifications, which made *my* dreams come true. And I know the players are over the top about the new field; they love the tight knit of the grass and the soil, which makes the field faster for them. They don't miss the old field for a minute.

Now I've always known that this new field wasn't just for the Patriots, but that it would have a variety of uses for sports and entertainment. I just didn't know entertainment would literally come first.

Two weeks before the Patriots were to play their first game in the new stadium, none other than the Rolling Stones arrived to set up for the first show of a major American tour. Because it was the first show, the stages and structures had to be newly built and assembled right there on my field. This whole process took eight days, with another

(continued)

three days of rehearsals, all for a Friday night performance that didn't even last three hours. For the entire 11 days, I covered my field with Terraplas, which protects the grass but allows UV and oxygen in through tiny pores in the material. Thanks to the Terraplas, it wasn't like a Woodstock nightmare or anything but still, I was pacing around watching them for days and sweating bullets.

The Stones' crew didn't finish packing up until 4:00 the next morning, at which time we had 12 hours to get the field in shape for the Revolution, who were to play the Major League soccer championship game that Saturday night. The Revolution won, which was good, of course, but then my crew and I had not quite 48 hours to get ready for the first Patriots game on the field, which was to debut on national television for *Monday Night Football*.

The field was in better shape than you might imagine, though all that action and pressure on the grass certainly took its toll. There were dings and flaws that *I* could see, especially in one of the end zones, but it was nothing a little extra field paint and logo action couldn't camouflage. And it looked good on TV, which is really all that matters, isn't it?

Here's what I know for sure about professional sports groundskeeping:

1. You have to know your field—your grass, your dirt, the contours, the tendencies—like the back of your hand.

2. You have to know your players' needs and requirements, and take them into account every time you work the field.

3. You have to love what you do. If you only like what you do, you don't have what it takes to be a professional groundsman in the bigs. You're married to your job, 24/7, for ten months of the year—you better love it.

Dennis Brolin

Head Groundskeeper

Gillette Stadium

Foxboro, Massachusetts

Lawn Games

Lawn games have been played for hundreds of years. What better way to enjoy your lawn than to play a few rounds of croquet or horseshoes? With a few pieces of equipment and your lawn as your playing field, everyone can enjoy an afternoon of fun.

Croquet

A classic fair-weather game, croquet can be set up on any good-sized piece of lawn. Although a regulation-size croquet course is 105 x 84 feet, you can use a 30 x 60 feet area for a good round of play. Even smaller areas are just fine for a quicker game. Play on shorter grass to keep the ball rolling as the longer grass will slow it down and slow down your game. Rearrange the stakes and wickets after you've played a course for a few times just to keep the game interesting.

Badminton

You'll need an area of about 20 x 44 feet for a badminton court, plus an extra 5 to 10 feet around the edges so players can move around out of bounds. Don't set up your court right against a fence or building or you'll have players bouncing off the walls to get the birdie—not exactly regulation play and not exactly safe. Mark all of the anchor ropes with a bright piece of string so the players know where they are and can avoid them. If you keep the net up all summer, be sure to aerate the area to reduce soil compaction and improve moisture absorption.

Horseshoes

For a round of horseshoes you'll need a strip of lawn about 6 x 50 feet, with a sand pit at each end. Making the sand pits is a bit labor intensive, so you can just place the stakes at either end of the pit without sand, but those heavy horseshoes can put some serious dents in your lawn. When you're done with the game, be sure you pick up all the horseshoes before you mow.

Football and Baseball

What would be more fun than to map out a smaller version of a football or baseball field in your backyard for a kid's birthday party? Use noncaustic (so it won't hurt your lawn) marking lime or line paint to draw the field. Marking lime is used with a line-marking machine (both available at sporting goods stores) that spreads the lime in a narrow line to outline the field. The marking lime will just get worn into the lawn over time. Line paint, available at larger sporting goods stores, doesn't hurt the lawn, or you can buy white latex paint and brush it on. Once the grass grows out, you just mow off the paint with the grass.

Tricks of the Trade: Homemade Snow Buddy

Where I come from in Ohio, the high school football season is well over by Thanksgiving. Where I live now, in New England, high school football rivalries are playing themselves out almost everywhere on Thanksgiving Day. Which means, in New England, there's often snow already on these modest fields and no easy way to remove it. I saw enough snow when I worked for the Green Bay Packers to last a lifetime and I'll never forget a trick George Toma taught me about getting snow off a field without damaging it.

Take PVC piping the length of your tractor plow, cut a slit in it, then snap it on the bottom of your plow, attaching it with bolts. Move across the field following the contours of your grass and you'll get the snow out of your way without tearing up the turf. Chances are you won't ever have to try this out on your own lawn, but you may have the chance to save the (snowy) game day in your hometown.

David Mellor

Putting Greens (and don't pretend you don't wish you had one)

Constructing and maintaining your own putting green isn't an easy task at all. Unless you'll be truly dedicated to your green, use the money for your local course greens fees instead. I can't talk you out of doing it, so how do you go about making what will be the envy of every other golfer in the neighborhood? Here's how.

1. Location, location, location. Your putting green should be placed in full sun, in an area with good air circulation, and mostly level with no depressions or low spots that will collect water.

2. You're essentially going to renovate the lawn in the putting green area. The putting green's performance will ultimately depend on the quality of its construction. You can't just mow the existing grass short—you'll just kill the grass. Check with the USGA for golf course green construction standards.

3. Let it rain on the area or water it thoroughly to find any low spots. Fill in those spots and be sure the water drains off the green in more than one direction to avoid ruts in the soil.

4. There are only certain types of grass you can plant for a putting green. Bentgrass (cool season) and Bermuda grass (warm season) are the only kinds of grass that can handle the extremely short mowing required for a putting green. Plant either type of these grasses that the golf course superintendents in your area recommend.

5. Tend to your new lawn as suggested in chapter 2.

If you don't want to do all that work to create your own putting green, you can always hire a professional to do the work for you. There are companies that will come out and set up a putting green to your specifications. You can just sit back and let the experts go to it. Look up landscape architects or landscape designers in your area to find a firm to handle your putting green installation. There are even companies out there that will install an artificial grass putting green. But really, what's the point of that?

Once your putting green is established, the *real* work begins. Here are some of the things you'll need to know to keep your putting green up to par.

Mowing

Mowing the grass on your putting green is not to be taken lightly. It is the single most important part of putting green maintenance. The whole point of a putting green is to get the ball to roll to the cup, and it can't roll if the grass isn't just right. You need to mow the grass between 3/16 and 1/2 inch high. You'll have to have a reel mower to cut the grass so close. The green should be mowed four or more times a week to ensure you're not cutting off more than 1/3 of the blade at a time. Keep your mower blades sharp at all times for a nice, clean cut.

Watering

Water the grass early in the morning and only when the grass is showing signs of drought. Overwatering such short grass can cause damp conditions that are ripe for weeds and disease.

Fertilization

Fertilize your putting green grass separately from your regular turfgrass. You don't want to apply too much nitrogen—just enough to keep the grass dense and green without promoting too much growth. Apply 1/2 to 1 pound of slow-release nitrogen fertilizer twice a season. Apply other nutrients as needed per the recommendations from a soil test on your putting green soil.

Tricks of the Trade: So You Think You Want a Putting Green?

People often ask me about installing putting greens in their backyards. My first response is, "Have you ever noticed that there are no golf course superintendents with putting greens in their backyards?"

If you choose to install a putting green:

1. Pick a sunny location with at least eight hours of sunlight from spring through fall. Morning sun is most important.

2. Be prepared to buy a bona fide greensmower—you can buy one used, which is preferable because of the prohibitive cost of a new machine.

3. Be prepared to mow at least five days per week.

4. Build it to the USGA standard of green construction.

5. Select the right variety of turfgrass for your area—consult a local golf course superintendent for varieties that will work in your area.

6. Install an automatic irrigation system.

7. Become aware of nutritional and pesticide needs of the turfgrass—and it will have needs.

8. Become friends with a good golf course superintendent.

9. Be prepared to travel less.

Brad Kocher

Golf Superintendent

Pinehurst Country Club

Pinehurst, North Carolina

Fungicide and Disease Control

Your putting green is high maintenance and should be treated as a microclimate unto itself. The different grass varieties and mowing practices used for the green will require different treatment than the rest of the lawn.

Topdressing

Applications of topdressing—a thin layer of compost—help break down thatch, improve drainage, and fertilize the green. Put down a ⅛-inch layer of compost and work it in gently with a push broom to be sure it gets down under the grass blades.

After all of your hard work, now's the time to relax and enjoy your lawn. Throw a party, play some games, or destress with a putting session. Or just get out there and wiggle your toes in your healthy, luxurious turf.

RESOURCES

A.M. Leonard, Inc. *www.amleonard.com*

American Lawn Mower Company *www.reelin.com*

Aqua-Maxx *www.aqua-maxx.com*

Audubon Society *www.audubon.org*

British Lawnmower Museum
www.dspace.dial.pipex.com/town/square/gf86/

Budd Seed *www.turf.com*

Care for the Environment While Caring for Your Lawn
www.magicouncil.org

Environmental Protection Agency *www.epa.gov*

Extension Agencies *www.reeusda.gov/hrd/statedir.htm*

Gardens Alive *www.gardens-alive.com*

Greenlink *www.greenlink.org*

Harmony Farm Supply *www.harmonyfarm.com*

IIome Depot *www.homedepot.com*

Hunter Irrigation *www.hunterirrig.com*

Husqvarna *www.husqvarna.com*

Intellicast *www.intellicast.com*

John Deere *www.deere.com*

Lowe's *www.lowes.com*

National Gardening Association *www.garden.org*

National Parks and Conservation Association *www.npca.org*

National Turfgrass Evaluation Program *www.ntep.org*

National Weather Service *www.nws.noaa.gov*

Ohio State University weather site *www.asp1.sbs.ohio_state.edu*

Professional Lawn Care Association of America *www.plcaa.org*

Rain Bird Consumer Products *www.rainbird.com*

Simplicity Manufacturing *www.simplicitymfg.com*

Snapper *www.snapper.com*

The Scotts Company *www.scottscompany.com*

The Toro Company *www.toro.com*

The Weather Channel *www.weather.com*

Turf Tips *www.agry.purdue.edu/turf/tips*

Turfgrass Resource Center *www.turfgrassod.org/trc*

Turfgrass Weeds *www.colostate.edu/Depts/IPM/natparks/turfweed.html*

United States Croquet Association *www.croquetamerica.com*

United States Department of Agriculture *www.usda.gov*

United States Golf Association *www.usga.org*

Water Environment Federation *www.wef.org*

World Weeds Database *www.w3.to/weeds*

INDEX

Page numbers in *italics* refer to illustrations.